Calm Down! Learn To Program

Learn how to write your own computer programs that will run on a Windows computer.

JERRY GENTRY

(WAØH)

Calm Down! Learn To Program

ISBN: 978-1-7321640-2-4

Printed in the United States of America

==

Table of Contents

==

==

Preface

==

A desktop or laptop computer is a pretty neat hunk of junk. It can hold down a stack of papers, it can make a soothing whirring noise, and it can partially heat a small room. If a computer contains things called computer programs, also called software, then it can do even more things.

A *computer program* is nothing more than a string of commands, written in a language that the computer can understand, that tells the computer what to do. A *boot* program tells the computer what to do when we turn it on. An *operating system* program is like the boss program. It runs other computer programs and controls things like the printer. The three main operating system programs are Windows, Apple Max OS, and Linux. *Application* programs tell the computer how to give us hours of joy and frustration. For example, a *word processing* program allows us to write letters. A *gaming* program allows us to waste time when we should be working. An *internet browser* program allows us to look up things on the internet such as why do software companies always want us to check that we agree to their terms and conditions when they know we are not going to read the conditions. And a *computer language* program allows us to write our own computer programs.

People who write these computer programs are called nerds, geeks, dorks, and sometimes *computer programmers*. If we want to make a lot of money or impress people, then we can call ourselves a software engineer instead of a computer programmer. If our boss does not want to pay us more money, then they will call us a coder.

I have been a computer programmer for almost 60 years, an old timer. The first couple of years I did not have much to do because they had not invented computers yet. Obviously, I think computer programming is fun. I find it rewarding to write a computer program and have the computer follow my commands and do exactly what I want it to do. I wrote this book to show people that learning how to write their own computer programs is easy. In this book I will show you how to get and use the tools you will need in order to write your own computer programs, and it won't cost you a dime, except for the money you spend on tums and aspirin. The tools we will use are called *Visual Studio* and *Visual Basic*.

No prior computer programming experience is required. You will need to have a desktop or laptop computer that is running the Windows operating system. You will also need to know how to do a few basic computer functions such as locating files and folders on your computer, copying files from one place to another, downloading and installing programs, etc.

Don't be intimidated by statements such as "To err is human, but to really foul things up you need a computer." It might be true that one misspelled word in a computer program that contains 100,000 computer commands could cause catastrophic events, but that rarely happens.

===

Acknowledgments

===

I would like to thank the computer programmers who wrote the tools that allow us to write our own computer programs. This includes the early programmers such as John Backus who in 1956 led a team of programmers at IBM to develop the programming language called FORTAN which is used to write engineering programs. And Dr. Grace Hopper who in 1961 led a team of programmers to develop the programming language called COBOL which is used to write business programs. I was one of Dr. Hoppers beta testers, seeing if COBOL would actually let programmers write their own computer programs.

I would also like to thank the more recent programmers such as Tim Berners-Lee who in 1990 led a team of programmers at CERN to develop the programming language called HTML which is used to write internet web pages.

My apologies to the many other programmers who helped create the hundreds of programming languages in use today.

On a more personal level, this book would not have been possible without the help of my wife of 53 years, Joan, who is a retired science teacher. I also want to thank my grandkids, Anderson and Kaeley, who always keep me in a good mood by laughing at my dumb jokes.

===

Chapter 1
GETTING READY TO PROGRAM

This is your last chance. After this, there is no turning back. You take the blue pill and the story ends, you wake up in your bed and believe whatever you want to believe. You take the red pill and you stay in Wonderland, and I show you how deep the rabbit hole goes.

From the 1999 movie - The Matrix

HARDWARE VERSES SOFTWARE

To most people, a computer is that thing that sits on a desk that we use to do things such as send emails, store pictures, balance our checkbook and look up things on the internet. Most people don't make the distinction, but a working computer is actually composed of two components, hardware and software.

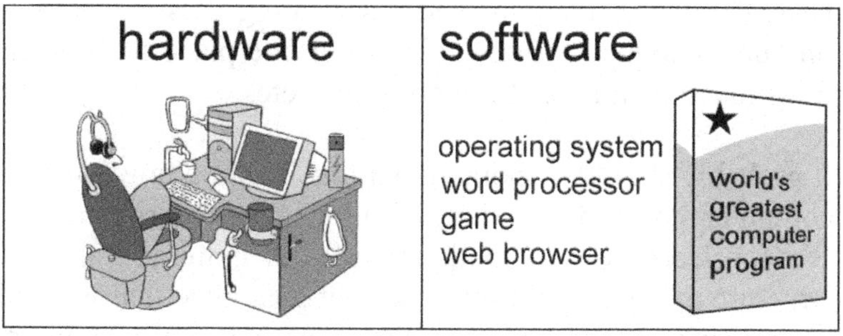

Hardware are the things we can kick when they don't work the way they should. Hardware consists of such things as the computer CPU box, the monitor, the printer, the keyboard, and the mouse.

Software are the computer programs, or apps, that we run on our hardware and when they don't work we call tech support at 3:00 am Sunday morning and get the message

"*Due to an unusually high call volume ...*". Anything the computer does is the results of a computer program telling it to do those things. An *operating system*, such as Windows or Apple OS or Linux, is a computer program that tells the computer how to start up, run other programs, and shut down. A *word processor*, such as Microsoft Word, is a computer program we can use to write letters. A *game*, such as World of Warcraft, is a computer program we can run when we don't feel like working. And a *web browser*, such as Chrome, is a computer program we can use to search for things on the internet.

In this book, we will learn how to write our own computer programs. The good news is that the process of writing our own computer programs won't cost us a dime, except for the money we spend on tums and aspirin. No prior computer programming experience is required. All we need to have is a computer that is running the Windows operating system. We will need to know how to do some basic computer functions such as locating files and folders on our computer, copying files from one place to another, downloading and installing programs, etc.

It probably should be pointed out that learning how to write computer programs is like learning how to write novels. We can learn how to spell, the rules of grammar, and the structure of novels, but that does not guarantee that we will become professional authors. For an author to write a novel they have to have a comprehensive idea of the story they want to tell. For a programmer to write a program they have to have a comprehensive idea of what they want the program to do.

Before we can learn how to write our own computer programs we have to know what a computer program is.

COMPUTER PROGRAMS

A computer program is nothing more than a series of commands, called lines of code, or statements, that tell the computer what to do. For example, consider the following computer program.

```
1 .. let (x) be the current time
2 .. if (x) is greater than 5 pm, then go to line 6
3 .. continue playing a game for 10 more minutes
4 .. let (x) be the current time
5 .. go to line 2
6 .. remind me that it is time to go home
```

The good news is that when a computer runs a computer program it does exactly what the lines of code tell it to do. The bad news is that when a computer runs a computer program it does exactly what the lines of code tell it to do. If we forget to include line 4 in our program, then the current time (x) will never get updated and we will never get to go home. When a computer program does not do what we want it to do we say there is a *bug* in the program. The term bug was first used in 1945 when a computer failed to work because a moth shorted out one of the vacuum tube relays in the computer. When we are trying to figure out why a program is not working we say we are *debugging* the program. I am currently in the process of inventing a new computer programming command, "*Do what I mean and not what I say*". When it is perfected it should cut down on the time we spend debugging our programs. Now that we know what a computer program is, how do we write one?

PROGRAMMING LANGUAGES AND COMPILERS

For any computer program to work the computer program (the lines of code) must be written in a language the computer can understand. The brain of a computer is composed of zillions of tiny switches. Each individual switch is either on or off. If we assign a value of 1 to a switch that is on and a value of 0 to a switch that is off, then all we have to do is translate our lines of code into a string of 0s and 1s. The language where characters are written as strings of 0s and 1s is called the *binary code*.

character	binary code
0	00110000 (really)
A	01000001
a	01100001
+	00101011

Since there are uppercase characters, lowercase characters, numbers, and punctuations, it takes at least eight 0/1 digits to uniquely represent each character.

> To learn more about the binary code and how to convert between binary code and alpha characters we can do internet searches for
>
> "*binary numbers and computers*" and
> "*text to binary converters*".

In 1959 I was a freshman at the University of Missouri. At that time, there were no such things as computer programming classes. Fortunately, I had a chance to work with a group of researchers who were using an old vacuum tube mainframe computer to try and find a better algorithm for finding the square root of a number. An *algorithm* is just a fancy word for a procedure. Most computers at that time were nothing more than number crunchers. To test our program, we fed in a number, coded in binary, and the computer displayed the answer, in binary coded lights, on the front panel of the computer. It was decades before the invention of keyboards and monitors. Fortunately, we no longer have to learn the binary code.

COMPILERS

Over the decades, computer programmers have written computer programs called compilers. This has given rise to the following jargon.

> A *programming language* is a language we use to write easy-to-understand lines of computer program code.
>
> A *compiler* is a computer program that translates easy-to- understand lines of computer program code into binary code.
>
> *source code* is what we call the easy-to- understand lines of computer program code.
>
> *object code* is what we call the binary code that comes out of the compiler.

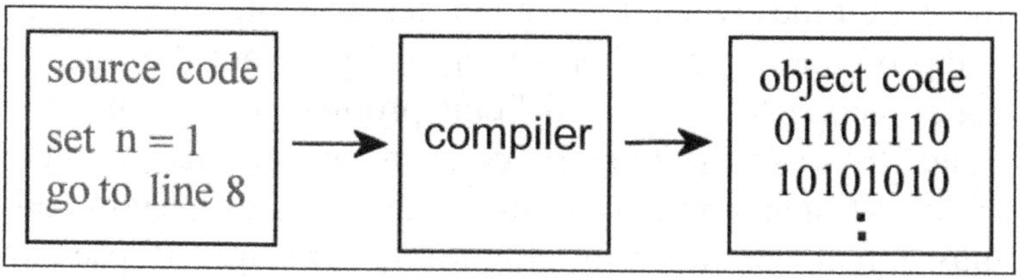

When we refer to a computer program we can mean either the source code version of the program or the object code version of the program.

Here are just a few of the more popular programming languages.

compiler	types of programs we can write
COBOL	business applications
Fortran	engineering applications
C, C#, C++	operating systems, games
html	websites
java	web apps, smartphones apps
objective c	apps for Apple computers
sql	database applications
Visual Basic	general purpose apps for Windows

It is common for a programming language and its associated compiler to have the same name. Visual basic refers to both a programming language used to write source code and the associated compiler that translates the source code into binary code. So what programming language did we use to write the six-line time-to-go-home program?

We can see that the language used to write the time-to-go-home program is not quite English. Not only are the lines of code not quite English, they are not a computer programming language. The language used to write those lines of code is called *pseudo-code*. Even though there is no compiler that will translates pseudo-code into binary code there are times when it is a good idea to write lines of code using pseudo-code. When trying to figure out the lines of code needed to solve a difficult problem it is sometimes easier to write the lines of code in near-English pseudo-code and then manually translate the lines of pseudo-code into a real computer programming language. If pseudo-code is not a real programming language, then what programming language are we going to use to write the programs in this book?

GETTING READY TO PROGRAM

To write the programs in this book, we will use a free programming language developed by Microsoft called *Visual Basic* or *VB*. At this time, the free version of visual basic is part of a package of Microsoft programs called *Visual Studio Community 2017*. Visual studio contains visual basic plus other programming languages such as *Visual C++*, *Visual C#*, and *JavaScript*. The visual basic part of the visual studio package contains both the visual basic programming language and the visual basic compiler.

INTEGRATED DEVELOPMENT ENVIRONMENT

To help us write books and letters there are computer programs called word processors. The word processor I am using is called Microsoft Word. To help us write computer programs there are computer programs called *Integrated Development Environments* or IDEs. An IDE will help us write our lines of source code, compile the source code, debug the source code, and run the program.

GETTING THE VISUAL STUDIO IDE

Before we write our first line of source code we need to download and install the visual studio IDE program. The visual studio IDE contains the visual basic programming language and the visual basic compiler program. Did I mention that they are both free? The next several steps show how to locate, download, and install visual studio. I hope this part of the book goes smoothly. There is a secret agreement among website designers, as well as companies that make computer programs, that whenever users start to figure out how to use their stuff they must change the way their stuff works.

HELP! What happens when things change a little and no longer work the way the book says they should work? Not to worry, thanks to the internet help is much easier to get now than back in the old days. Remember the old days, when we had to get up, walk all the way across the room, on shag carpet, just to change the tv channel. For videos on how to download and install visual studio we can search the internet.

If we do an internet search for "*download and install visual studio 2017*", we can find videos that show us step-by-step how to download and install the latest version of visual studio.

For other types of visual basic "*how-do-I*" questions, we can ask for help on one of several visual basic internet forums.

forum website
https://social.msdn.microsoft.com/Forums
http://www.vbforums.com
http://forums.codeguru.com
http://www.vbdotnetforums.com
https://www.devppl.com/forum/visual-basic-forum

We can't stall any longer, it is time to locate, download, install, configure, and learn how to use the visual studio IDE. To me, this process is as hard as learning how to write lines of source code. The good news is that we have to do this process only once.

To get the free version of visual studio we can do an internet search for "*download visual studio community 2017*". At the time I wrote this book, I used the following website.

https://visualstudio.microsoft.com/vs/community

Hopefully, a webpage similar to the following pops up.

On this website, click the (Windows) box and then click (Download VS Community). VS is the acronym for visual studio and VB is the acronym for visual basic. It should take only a minute to download visual studio 2017. Once the download is finished, go to the folder on your computer where programs are downloaded and double-click the file

vs_community_xxxxxxxxxx.xxxxxxxx.exe

Running (vs_community.exe) will start the installation process. Installing visual studio may take over an hour. The first screen to pop up is the Visual Studio Installer screen.

When the first Visual Studio Installer screen pops up, just click (Continue) to bring up the second Visual Studio Installer screen.

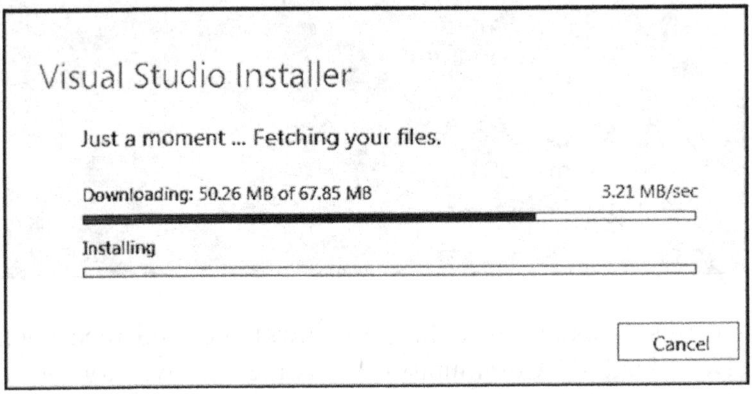

We don't have to do anything on this screen. After a minute the third Visual Studio Installer screen should appear.

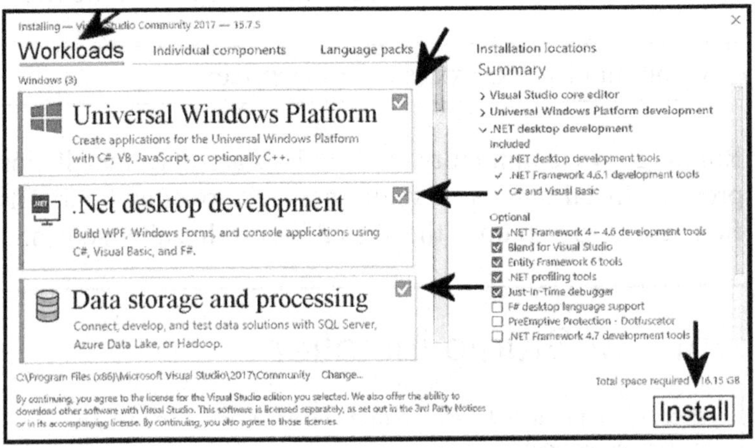

This screen allows us to configure visual studio based on the types of programs we want to write. For the type of programs we will be writing we just need to select the (Workloads) tab and then check the following three boxes.

Universal Windows Platform development
.NET desktop development
Data storage and processing

If we plan to use visual basic to develop more complex computer programs, then we can also check the following boxes. Since this is a book for beginners these advanced features are not discussed in this book but are easily found on the internet.

Web development - ASP.NET .. We can check this box if we plan to use visual basic to develop web application programs.

Azure development .. We can check this box if we plan to use visual basic to develop programs that save data to the cloud.

Mobile development .. We can check this box if we plan to use visual basic to develop programs that work on mobile devices.

If we want to add these workload components later we can do so by clicking the windows start button and running the program (Visual Studio Installer).

On most of the visual studio IDE screens we will use to write our computer programs, we can ignore 90% of the stuff on the screen. Ignoring that much stuff shows how powerful visual studio is. This does not mean the programs we will be writing are trivial. The stuff we will learn how to use is powerful enough to write most of the 65,000 lines of code that make up the MicroLog program I wrote for ham radio operators.

Once we locate and check the three boxes we can click the (Install) button which should bring up the next Visual Studio Installer screen.

This part of the installation process may take over an hour. When the installation is complete we should see the last Visual Studio Installer screen.

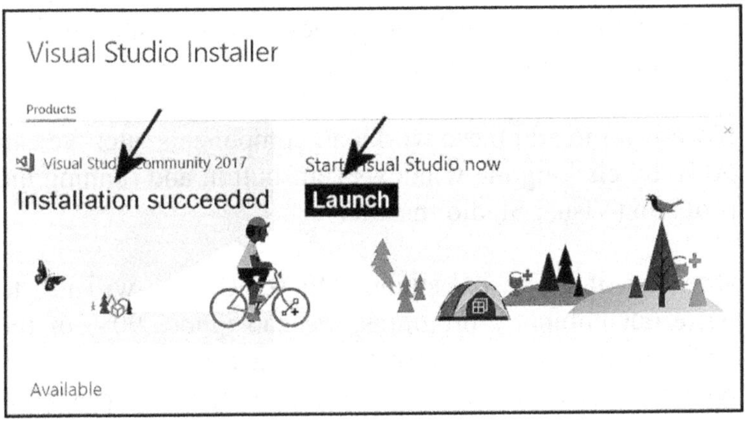

If the installation was successful we should see the words (Installation succeeded). All we need to do on this screen is click the (Launch) button.

At this point, we may or may not see the Visual Studio Welcome screen.

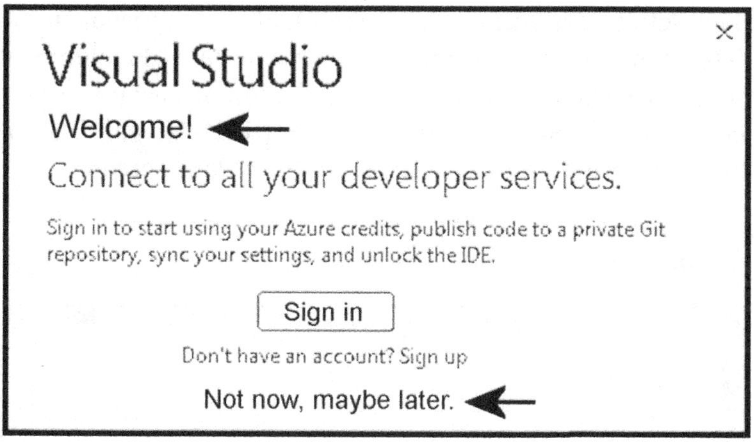

If we do see this welcome screen we can, if we choose, sign in to Microsoft using our Microsoft account. For the programs we will be writing it is not necessary to sign in, we can just click (Not now). We may get another sign-in option screen after 30 days. The final installation screen should be the Visual Studio familiar environment screen.

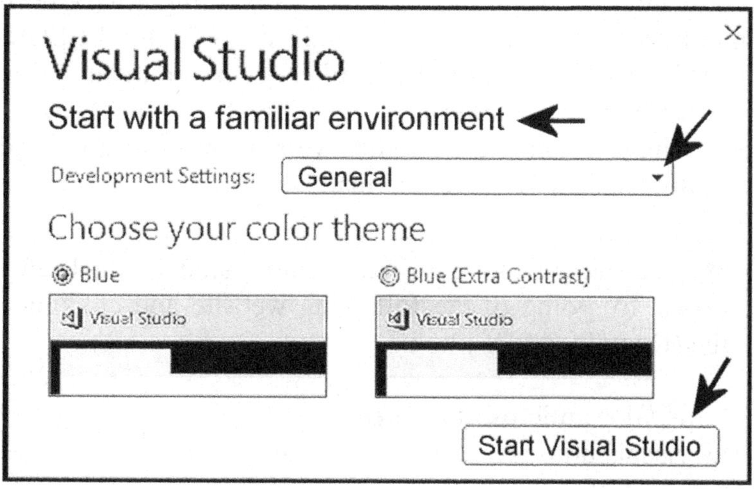

On the familiar environment screen, we need to click the black triangle to drop down the (Development Settings) box and then select (Visual Basic) instead of (General). This setting determines the overall look of the visual studio IDE window. If we forget to change the development setting we can do it later. The installation of visual studio is now finished so we can click the (Start Visual Studio) button to bring up the visual studio Start Page screen.

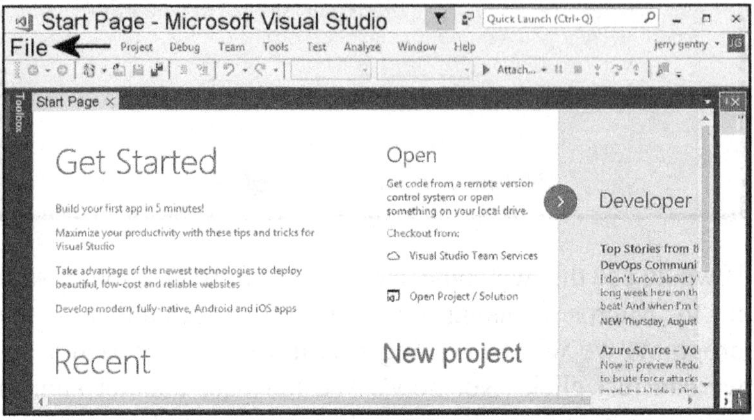

Since the installation of visual studio is finished we can close any leftover installation screens that might have been minimized. In the future, we can always bring up the Start-Page screen by clicking the word (File) in the menu bar at the top of the window and selecting (Start page). Since everything is running smoothly we may want to go ahead and download a visual studio manual.

> We can download a visual studio manual, all 1326 pages, by going to the following website and clicking the (Download PDF) link.
>
> https://docs.microsoft.com/en-us/visualstudio/ide/visual-studio-ide

CUSTOMIZING VISUAL BASIC

Before we jump into writing our own computer programs let's make visual basic easier to use by removing some of the features we don't need. The visual studio IDE window is divided into several sections. Most of the sections can be customized to fit our needs.

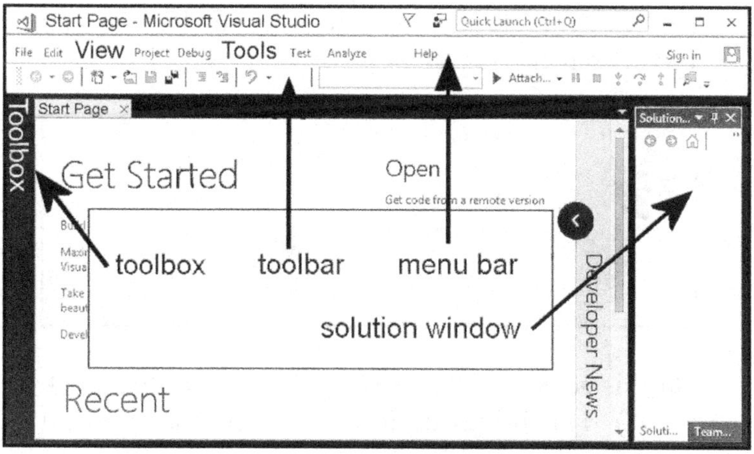

First, let's make sure the visual studio IDE is set up to write programs using the visual basic language. During the installation of visual studio, we had the option to change the Development-Settings from General to Visual Basic. This setting determines the overall look of the visual studio IDE window. If we forgot to change the setting earlier we can do the following.

> Click the word (Tools) in the menu bar and select (Import and export settings). This brings up the Import and Export Settings Wizard screen.

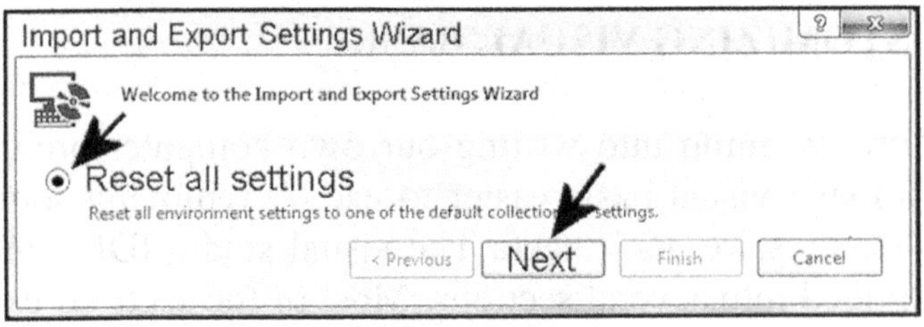

Check the (Reset all settings) button and then click (Next). This brings up the second Import and Export screen.

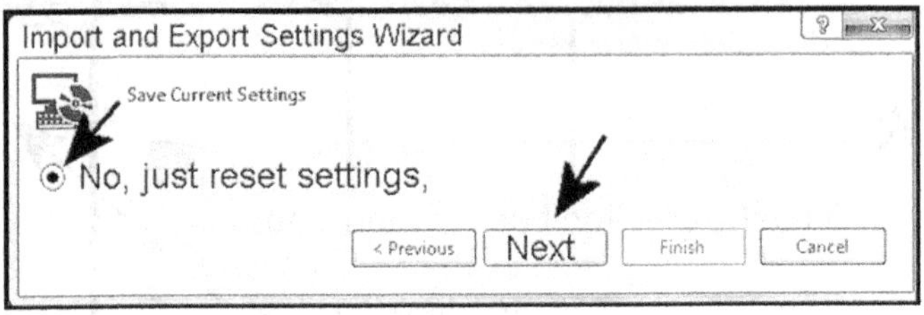

On this screen click the (No) button and then click (Next). This brings up the third Import and Export screen.

On this screen select (Visual Basic) and then click (Finish). When the reset is complete, click the (Close) button.

> To find step-by-step videos which show how to change the development settings to visual basic we can do an internet search for "*visual studio change environment settings*".

Other customization can be done by clicking the word (Tools) in the menu bar and then selecting (Options). This should bring up the Options window where we can make the visual studio IDE look and act the way we want. None of these customizations are required. The only reason for including this section is to show how to customize visual studio.

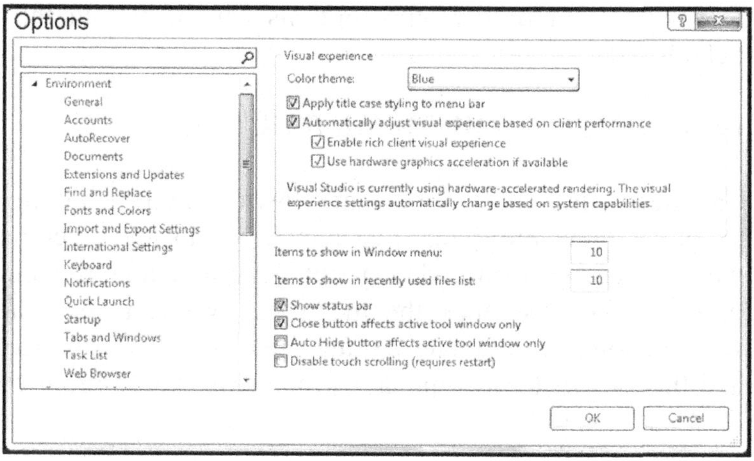

To start, let's change the size of the source code we type in our programs to size 14. To set the font size we can click the (Environment) tab on the left side of the Options window and then select (Fonts and colors). We can then select the type and size font we want to use to display the source code we write. After selecting the font, we need to click the (OK) button.

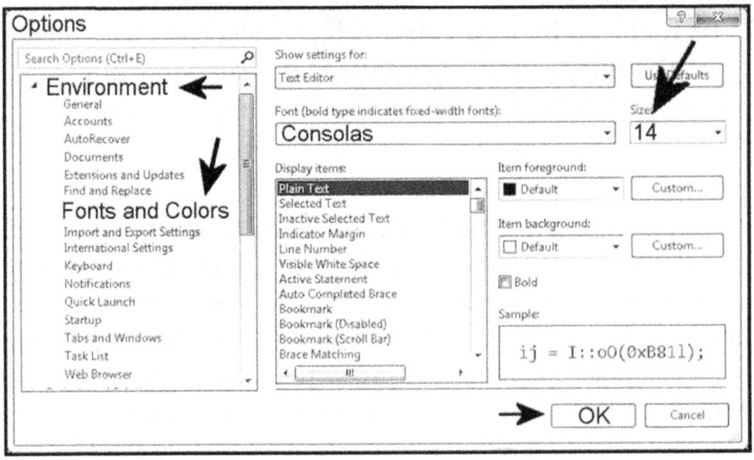

For now, most of the other options can be left in their default settings.

CUSTOMIZING THE MEMU BAR

The menu bar contains tools that allow us to do such things as start a new program, save our work, locate a certain word in our program, debug our program, and run our program. To customize the menu bar, we can click the word (Tools) in the menu bar and then select (Customize) and then select the (Commands) tab. This should bring up the Customize screen.

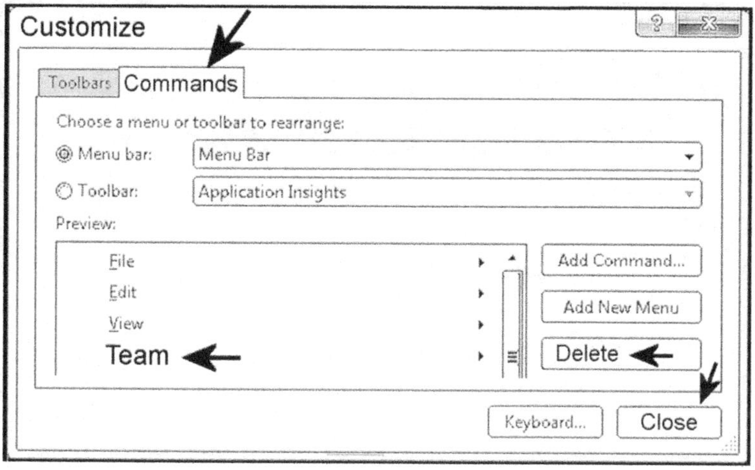

We will not need the tools in the Team menu so we can remove Team from the menu bar. To do this we can click the word (Team) and then click (Delete) and (Close).

CUSTOMIZING THE TOOLBAR

The toolbar contains icons that allow us to do the same things that the menu items do by simply clicking an icon. We can customize the toolbar by adding or removing different groups of toolbar icons. To customize the toolbar we can click the word (Tools) in the menu bar and then select (Customize) and then select the (Toolbars) tab. This should bring up the Customize screen where we can add or remove groups of icons.

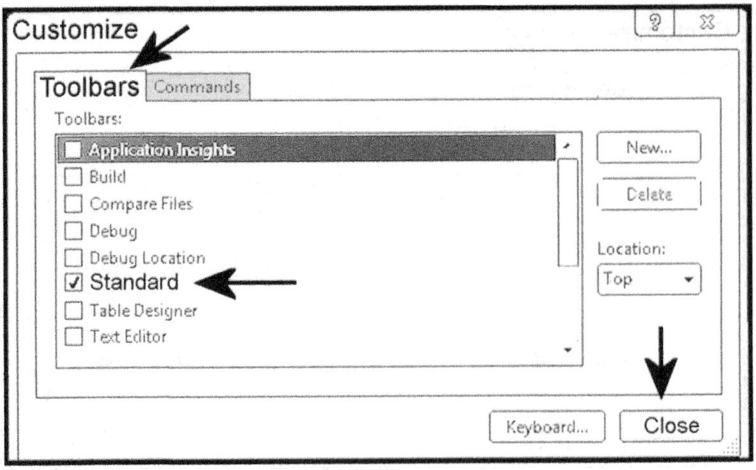

To add a group of icons to the toolbar we just check the checkbox for that group and then click (Close). At this time the only toolbar icon group we need is the Standard group.

CUSTOMIZING THE TOOLBOX

On the left edge of the visual studio Get-Started window is the word (Toolbox). If the word toolbox is not there we can click the word (View) in the menu bar and then click (Toolbox). Tools in the toolbox are called *controls*. Here are just a few of the controls we can add to our programs.

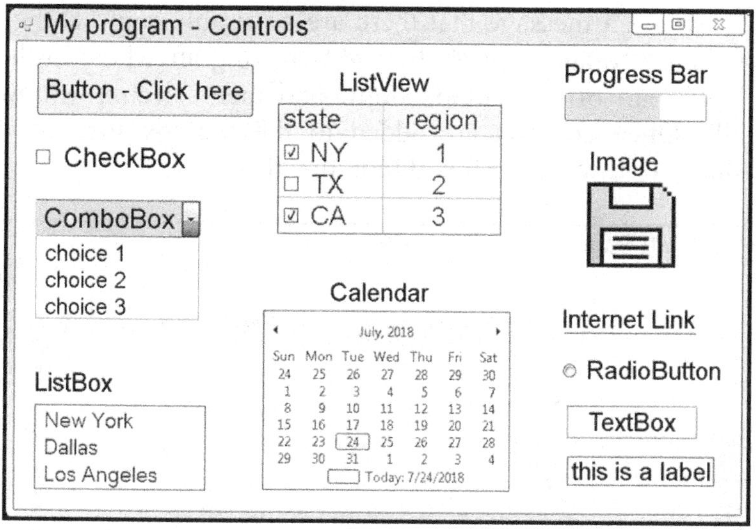

The tools in the toolbox allow us to add controls to our program. Controls are such things as boxes to type in, boxes to display things in, buttons to click, checkboxes to check, clocks, calendars, etc. The window we see when we run a program is a control called the *form* control. It could happen that when we click the word Toolbox we get the message "*There are no usable controls in this group*".

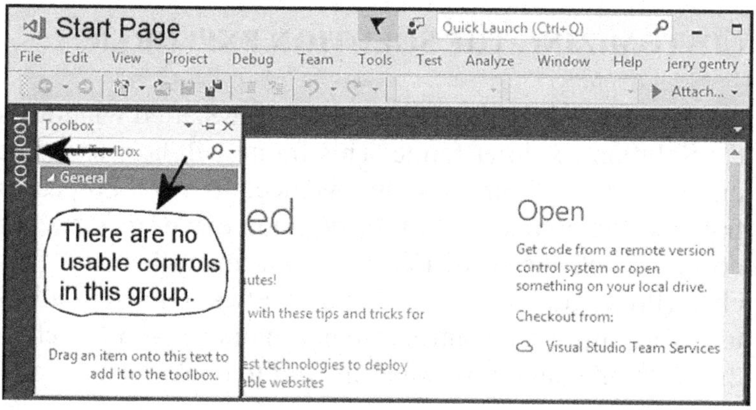

If we get a message that there are no usable controls then we need to add controls by right-clicking anywhere in the blank part of the toolbox frame and then selecting (Show all). Once controls are added to the toolbox the visual studio IDE window should look like this.

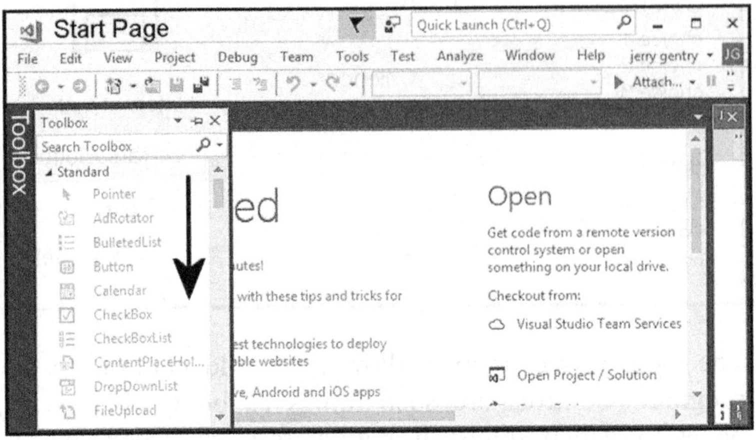

For now, don't worry if the controls seem grayed out or disabled. As with other visual studio features we will not need most of these controls. It could happen that tools don't appear in the toolbox until we start a new program.

CUSTOMIZING THE SOLUTION EXPLORER

On the right side of the visual studio Get Started window is the Solution Explorer frame. This frame will help us locate different parts of our program. We need to add a Properties frame to the bottom part of the solution explorer frame. To do this, click the word (View) in the menu bar and then click (Properties Window). The properties frame will allow us to customize the controls we put in our program, such as the color of a button we want the user to click.

Things in the solution-explorer frame do not show up until we are writing a program. Once the properties frame is added the visual studio IDE window should look like this.

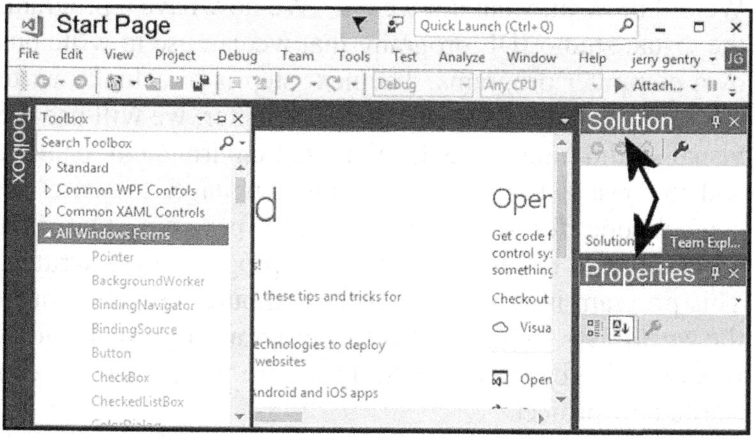

After all this work, we finally have the visual studio IDE program installed and customized. The visual studio IDE program will allow us to write our own computer programs. The good news is that we only need to go through this download, install, and customize procedure once. In the next chapter, we will fire up the visual studio IDE and write our first visual basic computer program. I would like to close this chapter the same way I closed the first chapter of my other book, "*Calm Down! It's Only Math*", by paraphrasing a quote from the 1997 movie "Men in Black"

> 1,500 years ago, everybody knew the Earth was the center of the universe. 500 years ago, everybody knew the Earth was flat. And 15 minutes ago, you did not know the steps needed to writing a computer program. Imagine what you'll know tomorrow.

==

Chapter 2
OUR FIRST PROGRAM

We did it! Wait, what did we did? We now have a program, the visual studio IDE program, that we can use to write our own computer programs. The next step is to actually write our own computer program. In this chapter, we will use the visual studio interactive development environment, or IDE, and the visual basic programming language, to write the source code for our own computer program. Our first program will be the most famous program ever written. This program is familiar to every computer programmer in the world. It is called the "*Hello*" program. In visual studio, programs are called *projects*. There are three ways we can start a new project.

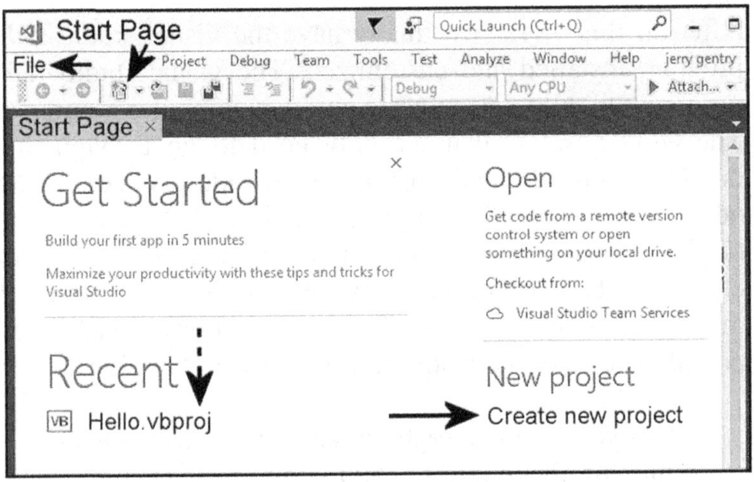

1 .. From the Start Page screen, we can click the link (Create new project).

2 .. From the Start Page screen, we can click the word (File) in the menu bar and then select (New project).

3 .. From the Start Page screen, we can click the New Project icon on the toolbar.

X .. If we want to continue working on some ProgramX that we worked on earlier, then from the Start Page screen, under the heading Recent, we can click (ProgramX.vbproj). The (.vbproj) file extension stands for VB-project.

No matter which new-project option we use to start our new program the New Project screen should pop up.

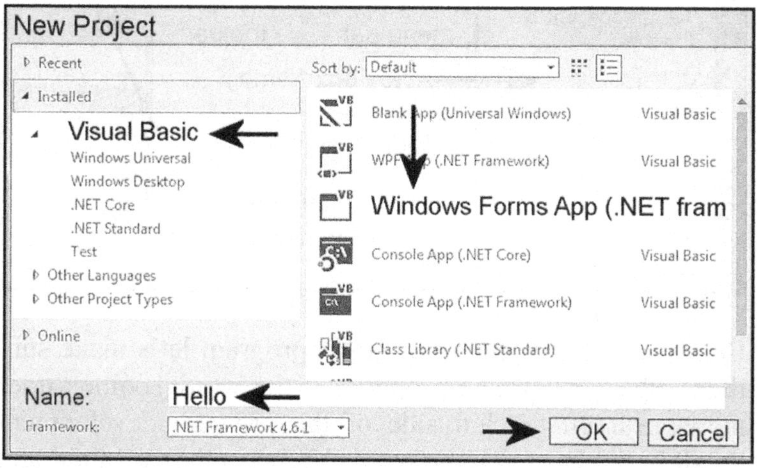

As mentioned in the previous chapter, it will be easier to learn how to write our own computer programs if we ignore most of the stuff on the programming screens and use only the stuff we need. It is sort of like buying the 74,608-page United States tax code and only needing to use 10 pages to do our taxes.

On the left side of the New Project screen, we want to select (Visual Basic). In the middle frame of the New Project screen, we want to select (Windows Forms App). For the purpose of this book, we can ignore the other choices. Near the bottom of the screen, on the line called (Name), we want to enter the name of our program. Let's call our program (Hello). We can now click (OK) to take us to the screen where we can write our Hello program.

THE PROGRAM DEVELOPMENT WINDOW

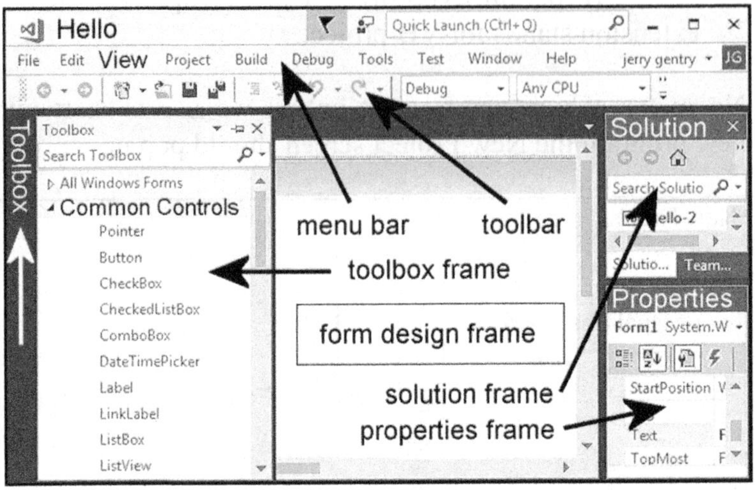

Before we start writing our Hello program let's make sure the toolbox is working properly. If the word Toolbox does not appear on the left side of the program development window, we can click the word (View) in the menu bar and then click (Toolbox).

If the toolbox frame says that there are no usable controls, then we can right-click in the toolbox frame and then click (Show All).

Most of the toolbox controls we need are in the group of controls called (Common Controls). The only control that is not listed is the *Form control*, the window we see when we run the program. For now, let's pretend the other groups of controls don't even exist.

THE FORM DESIGN FRAME

The center frame of the IDE window is called the *Form Design frame*. The form design frame is where we design what our program will look like when we run it. To make sure that not just anyone can become a computer programmer, us real programmers have created confusion by using the word program to mean both the source code we write that makes the program work and what we see when we run the program.

The image on the left is our Hello program from the standpoint of the source code that makes the program work. The image on the right is our Hello program from the standpoint of what we see when we run the program. In this section, we will learn how to use the form design frame to create the Hello program from the standpoint of what we see when we run the program.

For a small program, like our Hello program, it is helpful to see the whole program, or form control, inside the form design frame. To do this we can do the following.

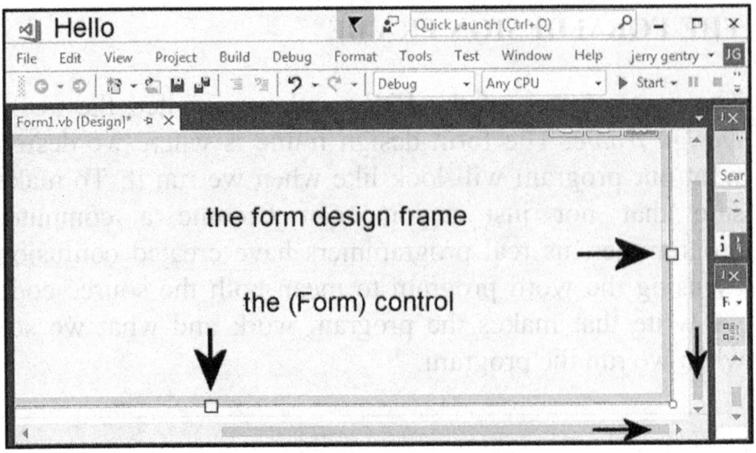

1 .. Click anywhere inside the form design frame and the toolbox will disappear.

2 .. Drag the bottom scroll bar all the way to the right and the right-side scroll bar all the way to the bottom.

3 .. Drag the little white dots on the edges of the program to shrink the program until it fits inside the form design frame.

CUSTOMIZING OUR PROGRAM

Let's start working on our Hello program by using the form design frame to design what we see on the screen when we run the program.

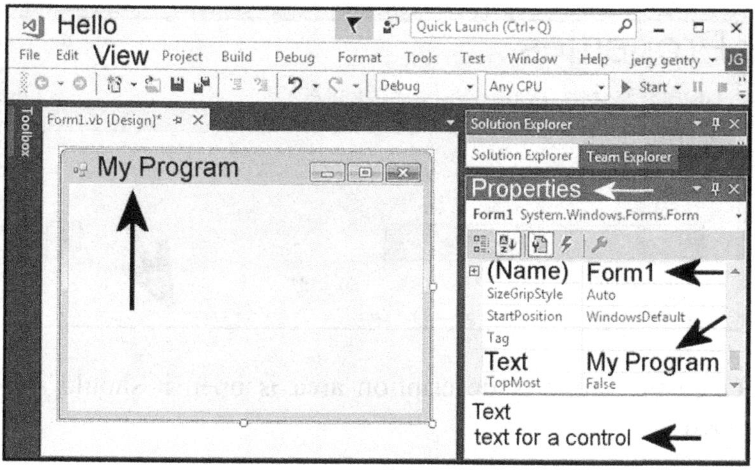

The lightly colored bar at the top of our program is called the *title bar*. Like any windows program, when the program is running we can use the title bar to move the program, shrink the program to the taskbar, or close the program. Since this is our program let's make the words (My Program) show in the title bar. To visual studio, and to the windows operating system, the name of the program is Hello. To the user who is running the program, the name of the program is the name in the title bar, My Program.

To determine how any part of our program looks we use the *Properties frame*. If the property frame is not showing we need to click the word (View) in the menu bar and then select (Properties Window).

If we click on a property line, such as (Text), a description of that property displays at the bottom of the properties frame. If the description area does not appear, then right-click any property and then click the word (Description). If that fails to show the property description, then use the mouse to drag the light gray line at the bottom of the properties frame upwards.

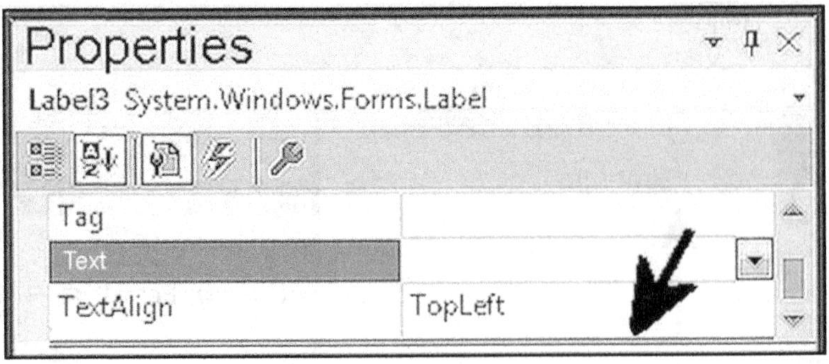

Once the property description area is open it should stay open.

To make the words (My Program) show in the title bar of our program click anywhere inside the form design frame and then go to the properties frame and type the words (My Program) in the line labeled (Text). Here are just a few of the other properties in the properties frame for the form control. For now, we can pretend the other properties don't even exist.

Name .. For simple programs that contain only one window, we can leave the name of the form control as Form1. More complex programs, such as a website that has multiple web pages, may contain several forms in which case each form will need a unique name.

BackColor .. We can use this property to set the background color of the program. Feel free to pick a background color you like. Sadly, the color and font size of the title bar is controlled by windows and cannot be changed.

FormBorderStyle .. We can use this property to specify how we want the border of the program to look and behave. Here are some of the possible settings.

None .. No border or title bar. This means there won't be any (x) in the upper right corner of the program so we will have to program another way to stop the program. A lot of games are designed this way.

Fixed single .. This is the setting used by most windows programs.

Sizable .. We can use this property if we want to be able to use the mouse to drag the edges of the program to adjust the size of the program.

Icon .. We can use this property to display our own icon in the title bar.

MinimizeBox, *MaximizeBox* .. We can use these properties to determine if the program can be minimized to the taskbar or maximized to fit the whole screen.

ShowIcon .. We can use this property to determine if we want the program to show an icon in the title bar.

Size .. We can use this property to determine how much of the monitor screen the program takes up when the program is run. If we want the program to take up the entire monitor screen, then we have to set the (WindowState) property to (Maximized).

StartPosition .. We can use this property to determine where the program will be displayed on the screen.

Text .. We can use this property to specify the words that appear in the title bar of the program. Since this is our program let's set the title bar text property to the words (My Program).

From the number of properties in the properties frame, we can see how powerful visual basic is. We have now determined how the program will look when we run the program. To finish our program, we just need to display the word Hello somewhere in the program. To do that we can use a control called a *Label control*.

LABEL CONTROL

The label control can be used to display text inside a program window. To put a label control in our program we can do the following.

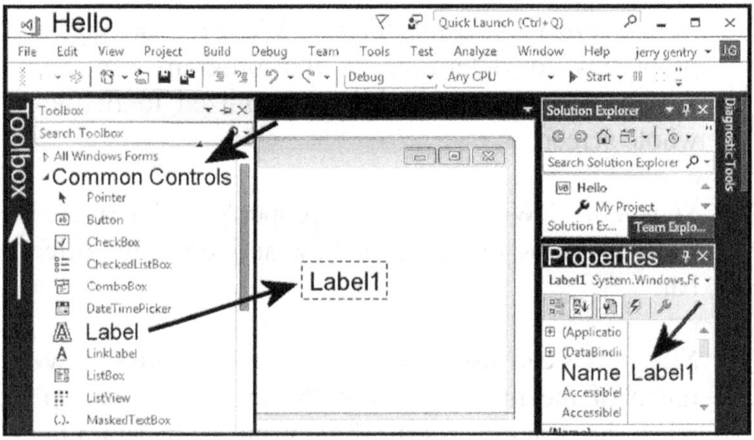

1 .. If necessary, click the word (Toolbox) to display the list of controls.

2 .. In the toolbox frame, click the word (Common Controls) to display the list of controls in that group.

3 .. In the list of common controls, use the mouse to select and drag the word (Label) to the form design frame. After releasing the mouse button, we can use the mouse to drag the label control to wherever we like.

Like the form control, the label control can be customized to look the way we want. To customize the label control, we click the label control and then set or change the properties in the properties frame. Here are some of the label properties we can set or change to customize our program.

Name .. Since this program has only one label we can leave the name of the label as Label1. Normally a program has several labels so each label must be given a unique name.

AutoSize .. If this property is set to True, then the size of the label box will expand to match the text that is displayed in it.

BackColor, *ForeColor* .. We can use this property to sets the background and foreground colors of whatever text is displayed in the label box. Feel free to pick colors you like.

BorderStyle .. We can use this property to specify if we want the label box to have a border.

Font .. We can use this property to specify the font type and font size of the characters displayed in the label box.

Size .. We can use this property to determine a fixed width and height for the label control. To specify a width and height just click the (+) sign.

Text .. We can use this property to specify the text that is displayed in the label, the default text is the name of the label control, in this case, Label1. We could change the text property of the label control to the word Hello and the program would be finished. The problem is, we want to become computer programmers and to be a computer programmer we have to write lines of source code. So, for now, let's leave the label's text property as Label1.

TextAlign .. We can use this property to specify if the text displayed in the label box should be left justified, right justified, or displayed in the center of the label box.

Visible .. We can use this property to hide the label box so that it is not visible.

SAVING OUR PROGRAM

It is always a good idea to save our program any time we add some new code to the program, make a change to the program's appearance, or test the program. The first time we save our program we must use the (Save All) tool. From then on we can use the Save tool to save the program. There are two ways to start the save-all process.

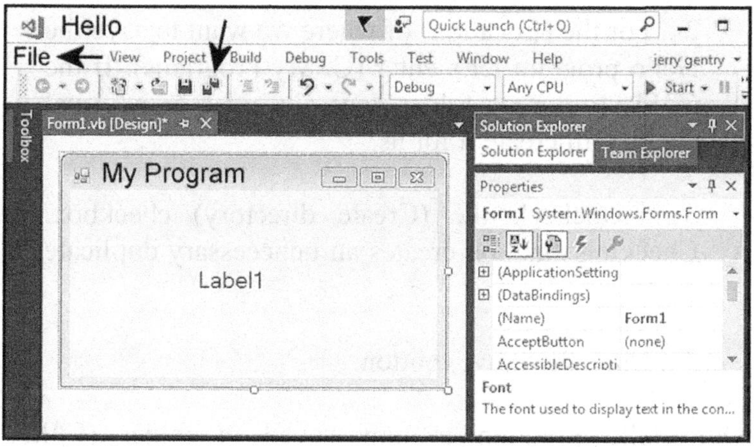

1 .. We can click the word (File) in the menu bar and then select (Save All).

2 .... We can click the (Save All) icon on the toolbar.

Either of these methods will bring up the Save Project window.

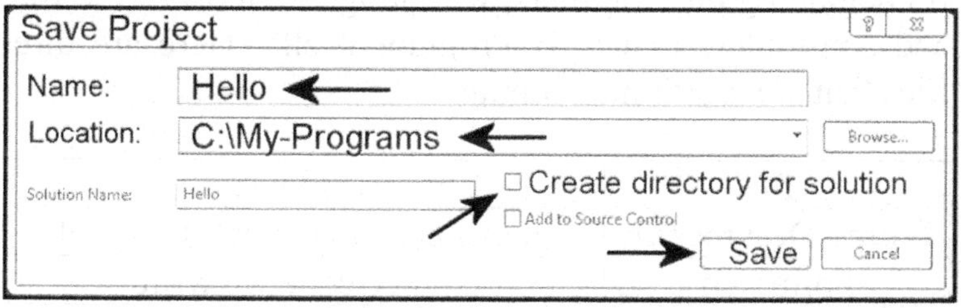

When the Save Project window pops up we can do the following.

1 .. For the (Name) of the program let's enter (Hello).

2 .. For the (Location) of where we want to save the Hello program let's enter (C:\My-Programs). If the C:\My-Programs folder does not exist, then visual studio will create it for us.

3 .. Uncheck the (Create directory) checkbox. Checking this box creates an unnecessary duplicate folder.

4 .. Click the (Save) button.

Our Hello program is now saved in folder (C:\My-Programs\Hello). From now on, to save the Hello program we just need to click the Save icon 💾. Since visual studio saves our Hello program in the Hello sub-folder of folder C:\My-Programs we can save multiple programs in the C:\My-Programs folder. Each visual basic program will be in its own sub-folder of C:\My-Programs.

When we first save our Hello program visual studio creates the C:\My-Programs\Hello folder plus some sub-folders. As beginning programmers, we can ignore most of the files and sub-folders of C:\My-Programs\Hello. Here are three files that are worth mentioning.

file	contents
Form1.Designer.vb	source code that creates controls
Form1.vb	source code we write
Hello.vbproj	the complete project

Any time we add a control, such as a label, to our program visual basic writes the source code necessary to create the control. Visual studio stores that source code in the file (Form1.Designer.vb). We programmers have to write the source code that interfaces with the controls, such as displaying the word Hello in the label control. The source code we write is stored in the file (Form1.vb). The file (Hello.vbproj) contains the entire project. If we double-click Hello.vbproj it will open the visual studio IDE and load up the Hello program.

Now that we have saved our Hello program we can test the program.

TESTING OUR PROGRAM

The normal procedure for writing a computer program is to add a few things to the program and then test the program to see if there are any bugs in the program. The more new stuff we add to the program prior to testing it, the harder it is to find a bug in the program. There are two ways we can test our program.

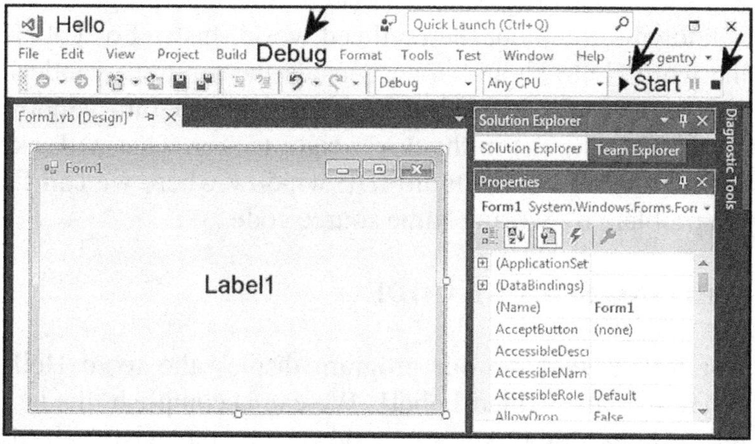

1 .. We can click the word (Debug) in the menu bar and then select (Start debugging).

2 .. We can click the Start icon ▶ on the toolbar.

If we want to stop a test we can click the Stop icon ■ to the right of the Start icon ▶. If there are no errors in the program, then we are rewarded with a view of what the program will look like when we run it.

When we test the program, the name in the title bar says that this is our program, but it is not the Hello program that is known throughout the civilized world. Instead of Label1 the word Hello should appear inside the program window. To fix the problem we need to close the program window by clicking the (x) in the upper-right corner. This will take us back to the visual studio IDE window where we can fix the problem by writing some source code.

WRITING SOURCE CODE

Our task is to have our program display the word Hello inside the label called Label1. We can accomplish this task by writing some source code using the visual basic programming language. When writing source code, we not only have to learn how to write the lines of code, we also have to learn where to put the lines of source code?

We just learned that when we save our program the source code is saved in two separate files. The source code necessary to create controls, which is automatically written by visual basic, is stored in the file (Form1.Designer.vb). The source code that interfaces with the controls, which we write, is stored in the file (Form1.vb). The visual studio IDE has two corresponding sections. The form design section is where we design the way the program looks when we run it. The code section is where we write the source code that interfaces with the controls in the program. So how do we switch back and forth between the form design section and the code section?

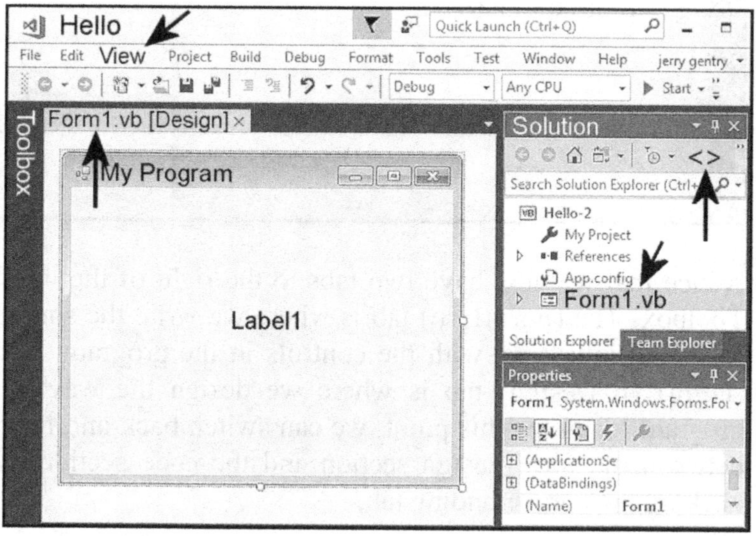

In the visual studio IDE window, notice the tab to the right of the word Toolbox. The tab we now have open is (Form1.vb Design). This is the area where we design our program. Always aiming to please, the visual studio IDE gives us a couple of ways to bring up the coding section.

1 .. We can click the word (View) in the menu bar and then select (Code).

2 .. In the Solution frame, we can select the line (Form1.vb) and then click the (< >) icon.

Either of these methods will bring up the coding frame where we can write our lines of source code.

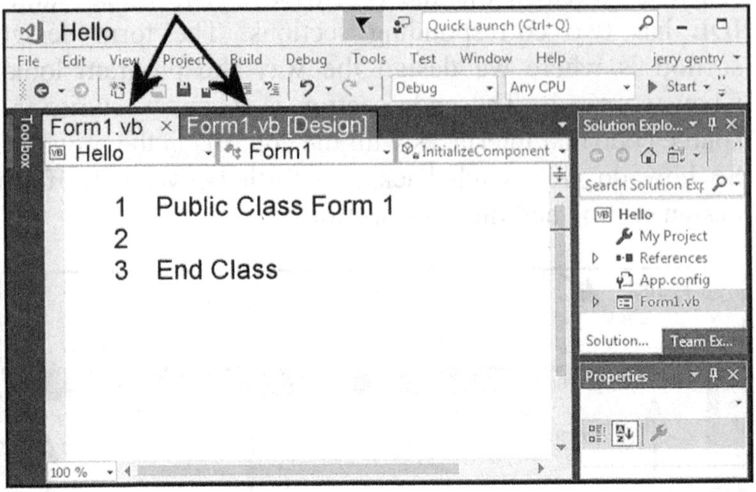

Notice that we now have two tabs to the right of the word Toolbox. The (Form1.vb) tab is where we write the source code that interfaces with the controls in the program. The (Form1.vb Design) tab is where we design the way the program looks. At this point, we can switch back and forth between the form design section and the code section by clicking the corresponding tab.

In the coding section notice that visual basic has written the first and last line of source code for us. All the source code we write will go between these two lines. For now, we do not need to know what these two lines of code do.

The only source command we need to write is a line of code that tells the program to display the word Hello in the label control. Since one of the properties of the label control is the Text property, all we need to do is set the text property of the Label1 control to the word Hello. Since there can be more than one label control in a program that line of source code will have to contain the name of the control as well as the property we want to set. When we want to set or change one of the properties of a control we use the following syntax or structure.

code to set or change a control property
name-of-control • name-of-property = whatever
Label1.Text = "Hello"

In a line of source code, any time we are referencing a group of characters, such as the word Hello, we need to use quotation marks around the characters.

Over my six decades of computer programming, I have discovered that when learning a new computer language, it is useful to create a cheat sheet of source code statements. The line of code above would make a good cheat sheet entry.

> IMPORTANT .. Any time we write source code it is critical that there are no spelling or punctuation errors.

Writing a line of source code is the easy part. Learning where to put the line of code is the tricky part.

WHERE TO PUT LINES OF CODE

The first guess as to where to put the line of source code that will change the text property of the label control to the word Hello would be on line 2, the line between Public Class and End Class. Let's put the line of source code there and see what happens when we test the program by clicking the word Start in the toolbar.

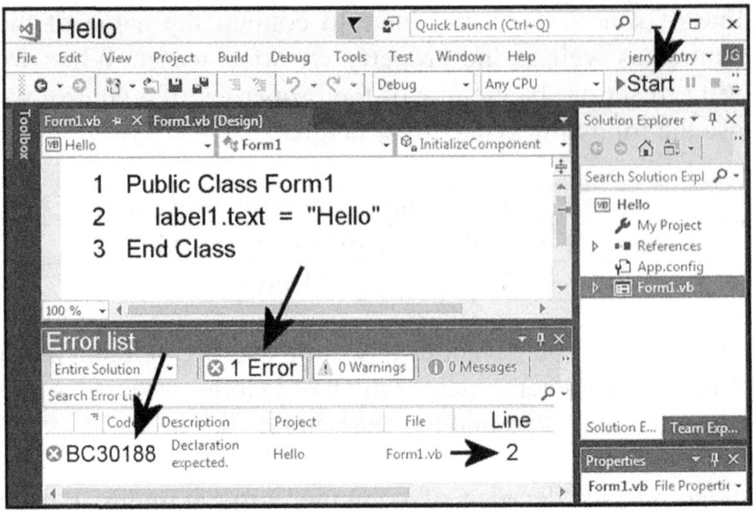

The test does not show us what the program will look like when we run the program because there is a bug in the program. The Error List frame says there is 1 error. Sadly, the explanation line is not all that helpful as to what caused the error. The status line does say the error occurred on line 2, the line of code we just added. Sometimes the internet is helpful in finding what causes a bug, but not in this case.

> If we do an internet search for "*visual basic what causes error code BC30188*", we can find that other programmers have wondered about this error but there is not much help as to what causes the error.

The fact is, there is nothing wrong with our line of code. The problem is, the line of code is in the wrong place. In the good old days, before desktop computers, we programmers wrote our programs line-by-line, starting at line 1 and ending thousands of lines later with an End Program line. Programs today are different. Programs today set idly by waiting for the *user*, the person who is running the program, to do something. When the user does something such as click a button, check a checkbox, or type something in a box then the program responds by executing a section of code. For this reason, the source code we write must be in a section of the program that is set aside to respond to something the user does.

An easy-to-understand example of responding to something a user does is displaying the word Ouch! whenever the user moves his mouse over a label control. We know that controls have properties, such as color, but moving a mouse over a label control is not a property of the control so it must be something else.

label control
Property .. an attribute of the control, such as its color
Event .. something we do to a control, such as click it.

Things that can happen to a control are called *events* of that control. We would therefore put the source code to display the word Ouch! in the section of the program that is set aside to handle the Mouse-Moves-Over event of the label control. When the user does something, and the program responds by going to a certain section of code we say the program *triggers* that event. In this example, moving the mouse over a label control triggers the Mouse-Moves-Over event of that control.

But wait, setting the text property of the Label1 control to the word Hello is a little different than the ouch example. In the ouch example, the user moves their mouse over a label control which triggers the mouse-moves-over event of that control. In the Hello program, the user just runs the program, they do not do anything to any of the controls. So once again, where do we put the code to set the Text property of the Label1 control? The answer is, in one of the events of the other control in the program, the Form1 control. The Form1 control is the screen we see when we run the program. The Form1 control contains other controls such as the Label1 control. When we run our program think of Windows as being the first user of the program and what it does is (load) the program, or (Form1) control, onto the monitor so we can see it. The question then becomes, how do we find the (Load) event of the (Form1) control?

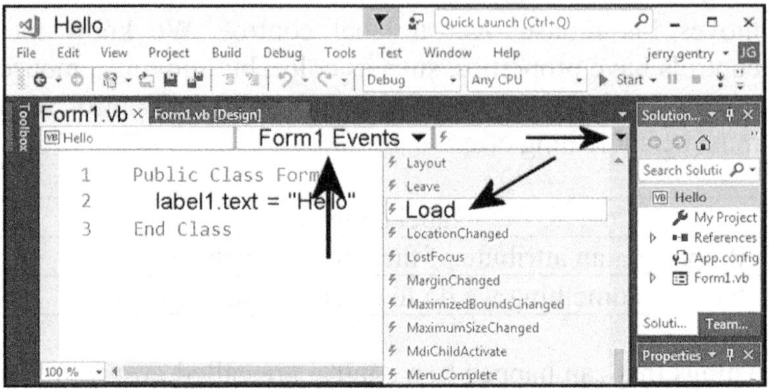

When we are in the code frame of the visual studio IDE there is a row of three boxes directly above the place where we write lines of source code. We use these boxes to find any event of any control in our program.

1 .. The middle box shows the names of the controls in our program. We want to click the black triangle on the right side of the middle box to drop down a list of controls and then select the (Form1 Events) control.

2 .. The box on the right shows the names of the events for the control shown in the middle box, the Form1-Events control. We want to drop down the list of events and then select the (Load) event.

When we select the Load event of the Form1 control visual studio will take us to the section of the program where we can add source code that describes what we want the program to do prior to displaying the program for the user.

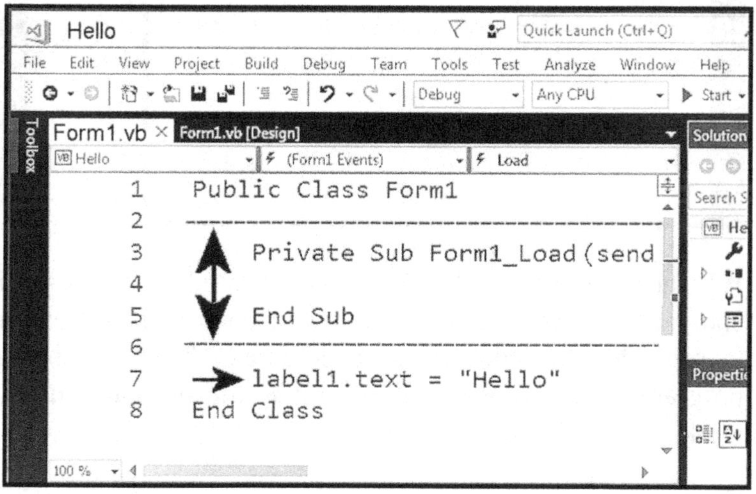

Ok, I lied. Visual studio does not actually take us to some other section of the program called Form1-Load. Instead, visual studio creates a little section of code called (*Private Sub Form1-Load*) and puts it in the main part of our program. We will learn about Private Sub or subroutines later. For now, we can ignore the words that are inside the parenthesis of the Private Sub line. We just need to know that a *subroutine* is just a little independent section of code and that any code we want done prior to displaying the program, such as setting the text property of a label, goes in the Form1-Load subroutine. All we need to do for the program to work is move the (Label1.Text) line from the main part of the program to the Form1-Load section of the program.

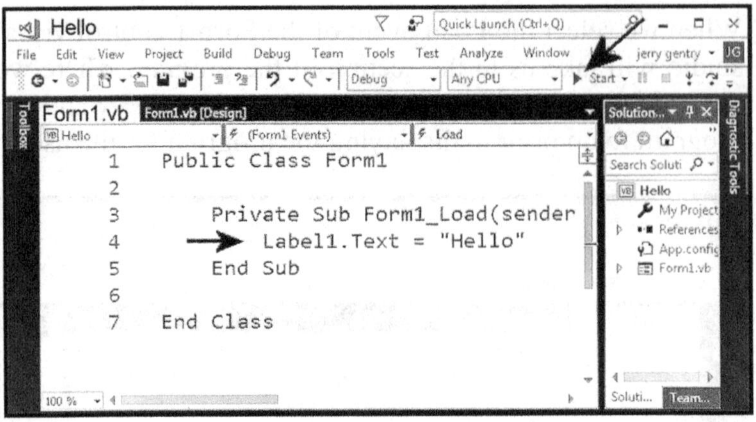

Whether the (Label1.Text) line is indented or not is your choice. Sometimes indenting lines of code makes it easier to see what the code does. This time, when we run the program by clicking the Start icon ▶ the program should work.

Congratulations, you have now written your first computer program. Welcome to the league of computer programmers, here is your CRAPPY award.

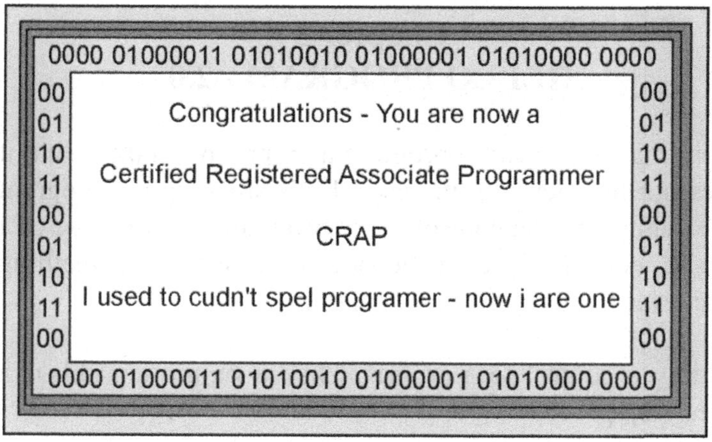

And if you are ever asked the question "*How many programmers does it take to change a light bulb?*", the answer is "none", changing a light bulb is a hardware problem and programmers write software.

Nobody wants to be a crappy programmer so in the next chapter we will learn how to spice up our programs. Let's finish this chapter by saving our program one more time.

1 .. Click the word (File) in the menu bar and select (Save All).

2 .. Or, click the (Save All) icon on the toolbar.

Once we have saved our Hello program we can close out the program from the visual studio IDE.

Click the word (File) in the menu bar and select (Close Project).

==

Chapter 3
HELLO PROGRAM - 2.0

What makes our Hello program a crappy program is that it does not interact with the user. Let's spice up the program by adding a button control to the program. The purpose of a button control is to have the program do something whenever the user clicks the button.

Adding a control to a program, like a button control, is a three-step process.

1 .. Add the control to the form design frame.

2 .. Set or change the properties of the control.

3 .. Add source code that the program will execute whenever the control is triggered. In this case, whenever the button is clicked.

BUTTON CONTROL

Since the last thing we did in the previous chapter was close out the program from the visual studio IDE, the first thing we need to do in this chapter is reload the project.

HELLO PROGRAM - 2.0

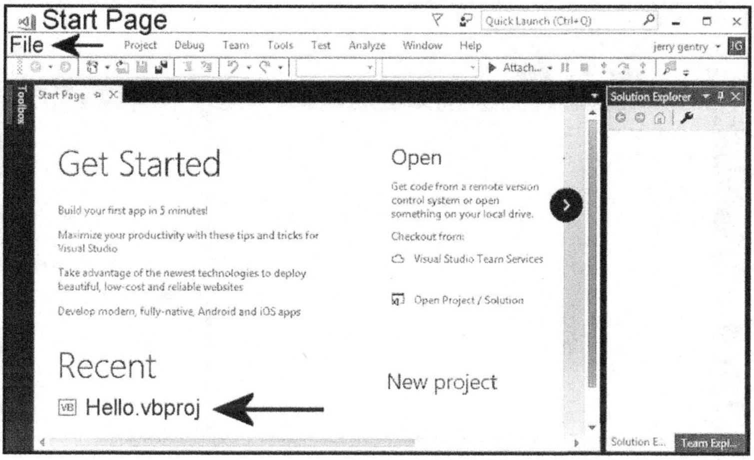

There are two ways we can reload the previously saved Hello program.

1 .. From the Get Started screen, under the heading Recent, we can click the link (Hello.vbproj).

2 .. We can click the word (File) in the menu bar and then select (Open Project). Visual studio will then ask us to locate and open the file (Hello.vbproj) which we previously saved in folder (C:\My-Programs\Hello).

Our Hello program should now be reloaded into the visual studio IDE. In order to add a button control to our program, we must have the form design frame showing.

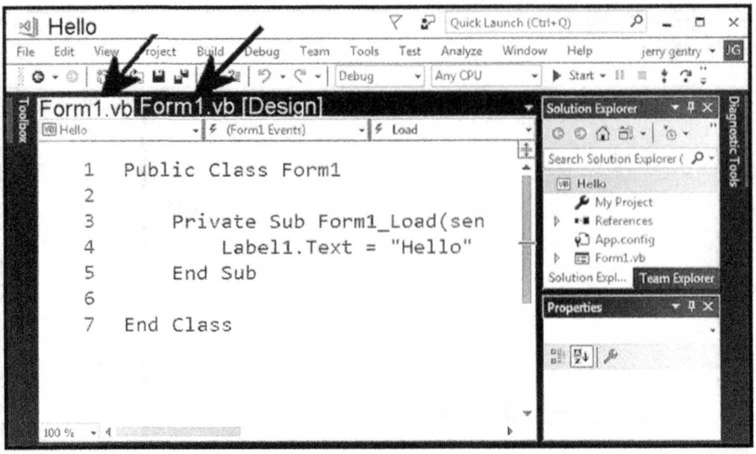

If the code frame is showing, which is under the (Form1.vb) tab, then we need to click the (Form1.vb Design) tab to show the form design frame. Once the form design frame is showing we can add a button control to the program.

The procedure for adding a button control to our program is similar to the procedure we used to add a label control to the program.

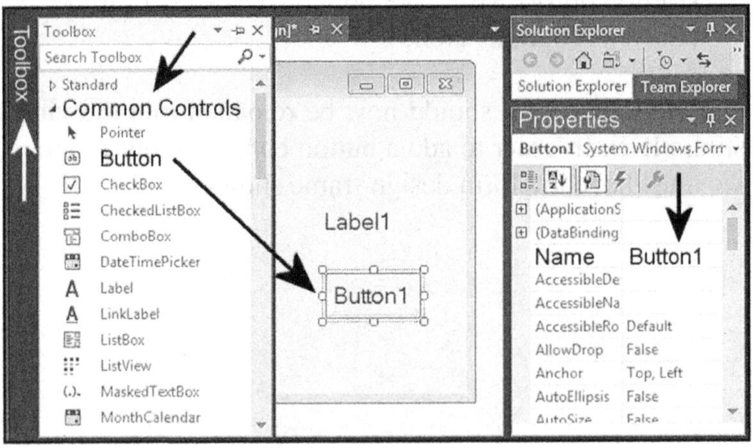

Do not be alarmed if the form design frame shows the word Label1 instead of Hello. In the previous chapter, when we added the Label1 control to the program, we left its text property the default value of Label1. In the program, specifically the Form1-Load section of the program, we used source code to change the text property of the label to Hello.

To add a button control to the program we can do the following.

1 .. Click the word (Toolbox) to display the list of controls.

2 .. In the toolbox frame, click the word (Common Controls) to display the list of controls in that group.

3 .. In the list of Common Controls, use the mouse to select and drag the word (Button) to the form design frame. After releasing the mouse button, we can use the mouse to size and drag the button control to wherever we like.

Like the label control, the button control can be customized to look the way we want. To customize the button control we click the (Button1) control and then set or change the properties in the Properties frame.

If the properties frame is not showing then we need to click the word (View) in the menu bar and select (Properties Window). If the property description area is not showing at the bottom of the properties frame then we need to right-click a property, such as (Text), and then click the word (Description). Once the description area is open it should stay open.

Here are some of the button properties we can set or change to customize the way the control looks and works.

Name .. Since this program has only one button we can leave the name of the button as Button1. Normally a program has several buttons, so each button must be given a unique name.

BackColor, *ForeColor* .. We can use these properties to sets the background and foreground colors of whatever text is displayed on the button. Feel free to pick colors you like.

Enabled .. We can use this property to disable the button under certain conditions. If a button is disabled then clicking it does nothing.

Font .. We can use this property to specify the font type and font size of the characters displayed on the button.

Text .. We can use this property to specify the text that is displayed on the button. The default is Button1. Let's change the text property to (Click here).

TextAlign .. We can use this property to specify if the text displayed on the button should be left justified, right justified, or displayed in the center of the button.

Visible .. We can use this property to hide the button under certain conditions.

We have now added a button control to our program and set its properties. Let's say that the reason we added the button control is that we want the program to replace the word Hello with (I said HELLO!) when the user clicks the button. So, where do we put the source code that will respond to the user clicking the button?

BUTTON CONTROL SOURCE CODE

When we used source code to change the text property of the label control to Hello, we put the code in the load event of the form control, or the Form1-Load section of the program. We wanted the code to be executed prior to the program loading. The place to put the code for the Button1 control is different. We don't want the code for the Button1 control to be executed prior to the program loading. We want the code for the Button1 control to be executed when the user clicks the button.

When we introduced the label control in the previous chapter we said that a control has properties, such as color, and events, such as clicking. We therefore want to put the source code for the button control in some sort of click event for the button control, or in a Button1-Click section of the program. When the user clicks the button, the program will trigger the Button1-Click event and execute the code in that section. As mentioned in the previous chapter, to find the events for a certain control we must be in the code frame.

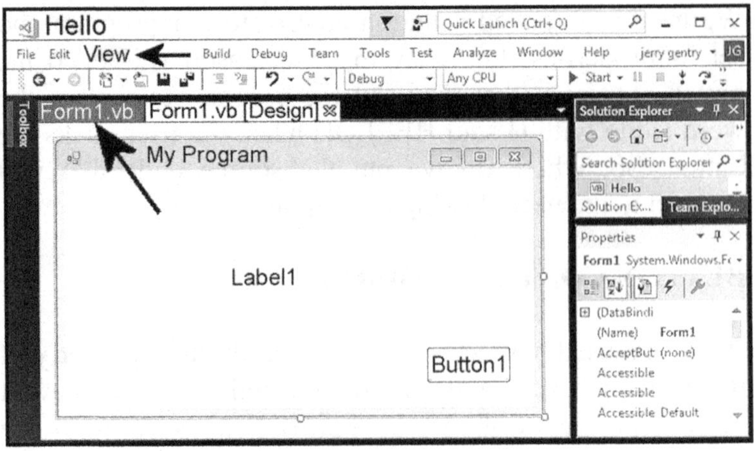

There are two ways we can switch from the form design frame to the code frame.

1 .. We can click the (Form1.vb) tab at the top of the form design frame.

2 .. We can click the word (View) in the menu bar and then select (Code).

Once in the code frame we can locate the click event.

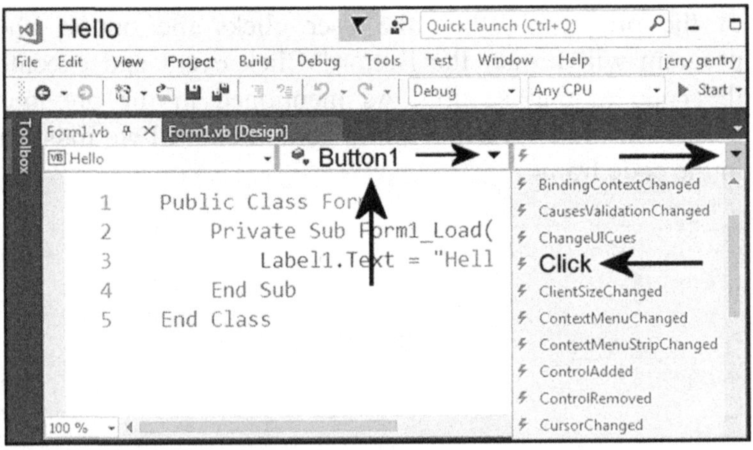

To locate the code section for the click event of the Button1 control we use the row of boxes located directly above the place where we write lines of code.

1 .. The middle box shows the names of the controls in our program. We want to click the black triangle on the right side of the box to drop down the list of controls and then select the (Button1) control.

2 .. The box on the right shows the names of the events for the control shown in the middle box, the Button1 control. We want to drop down the list of events and then select the (Click) event.

Once we select the click event the visual studio IDE will take us to the section of the program where we can add code that describes what we want the program to do when the user clicks the button.

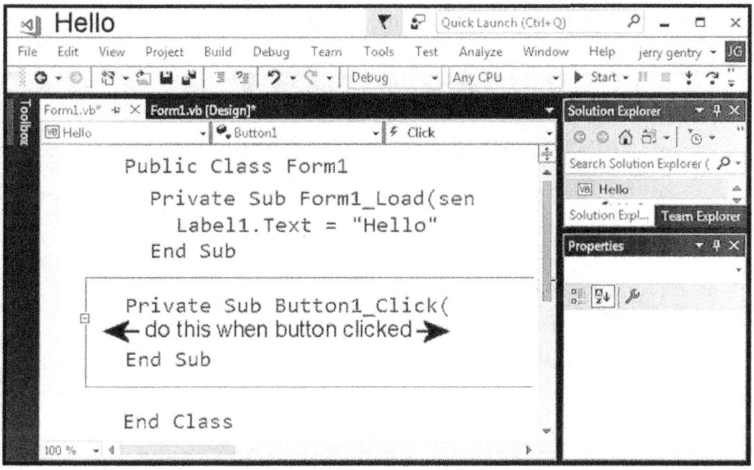

And once again I lied. Visual studio does not actually take us to some other section of the program called Button1-Click. Instead, visual studio creates a little section of code called (*Private Sub Button1-Click*) and puts it in the main part of our program. For now, we can ignore the words that are inside the parenthesis of the Private Sub line. Any code that we want to be done when the user clicks Button1 goes in the Button1-Click section. And once again, visual basic has written the first and last line of source code for us.

We now have the section of the program where we put the source code that will change the text property of Label1 from Hello to (I said HELLO!) when the user clicks the Button. When the user clicks the Button1 control let's also hide the button so they can't click it again. The two lines of code that do this are

Label1.Text = "I said HELLO!"
Button1.Visible = False

After we add the two lines of code to the Button1-Click event our program should look like this.

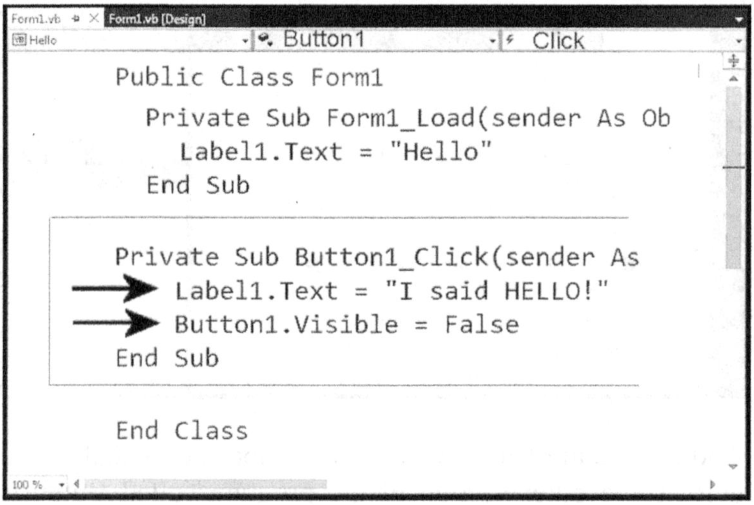

Notice what happens when we start typing the (Label1.Text) line of code. As soon as we type (Lab) a list of choices pops up showing all the visual basic code words that start with (Lab).

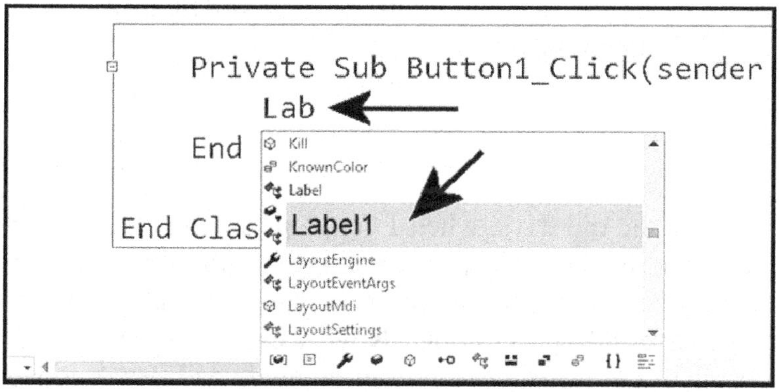

From this list, we can scroll down to (Label1) and press the spacebar. Visual basic will fill in the rest of the word. We can also type (Te), select (Text) from the list, press the spacebar, and let visual basic fill in the rest of the word. This is helpful when typing long statements.

Once again, notice how we write a line of code that is meant to change the property of a control. The syntax is (control-name) followed by a (period) followed by the (property value), or (Button1.Visible = False).

After we add the two lines of code we can test the program by clicking the Start icon ▶ in the toolbar.

before clicking the button	after clicking the button

Back in the old days, when I could sit down in a chair and get back up again without making a grunting sound, to learn a computer programming language we had to buy an expensive 800-page book. Now we can do an internet search for "*visual basic button control*" and watch videos on how a button control works.

Now seems like a logical time to introduce a line of source code that does nothing. A line of code that does not even get executed. A comment.

```
' This is a comment line .. it starts with an apostrophe
```

Comments are used to help us, or other programmers, figure out what lines of code do. Using comments, our program looks like this.

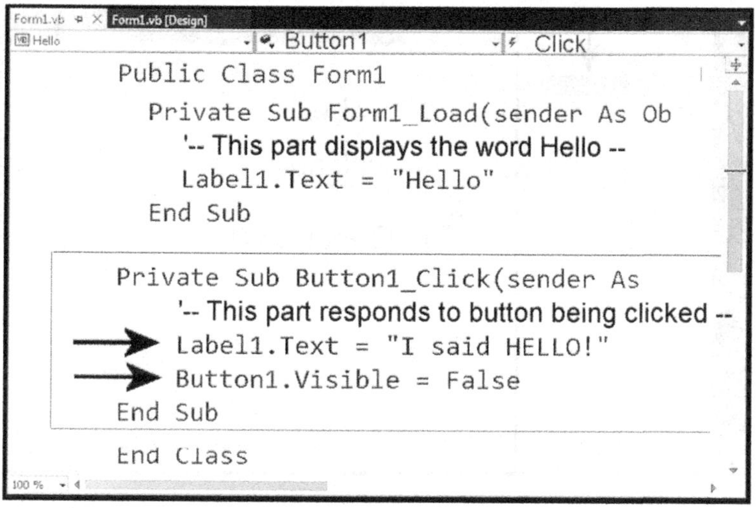

Our Hello program is beginning to look a little less crappy. Since we are on a roll, let's add a checkbox control to our program. The purpose of a checkbox control is to have the program do something whenever the user checks or unchecks the checkbox. Let's have our checkbox do the following.

> If the user checks the checkbox, then we want the program to display (Hello Hello) in the label control.

> If the user unchecks the checkbox, then we want the program to just display Hello in the label control.

CHECKBOX CONTROL

The procedure for adding a checkbox control to our program is similar to the procedure we used to add a label control and a button control to the program.

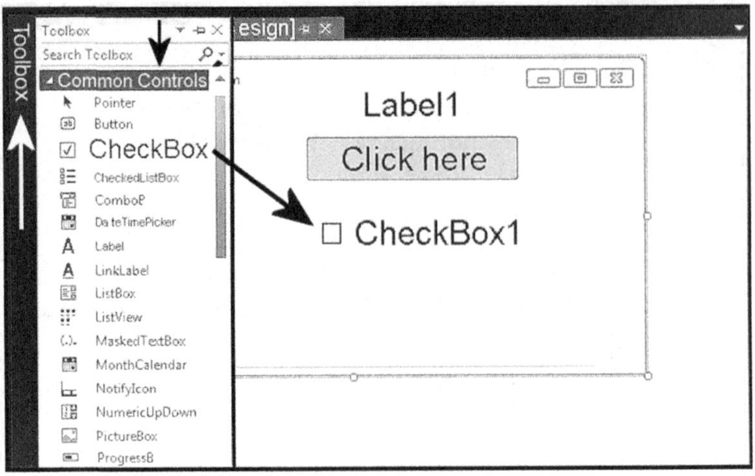

1 .. If the source code frame is showing, then we need to switch back to the form design frame by clicking the (Form1.vb Design) tab.

2 .. Once in the form design frame we need to click the word (Toolbox) to display the list of controls.

3 .. Once the toolbox frame is open we need to click the word (Common Controls) to open up that group of controls.

4 .. In the list of common controls, we can use the mouse to select and drag the word (CheckBox) to the form design frame. After releasing the mouse button, we can use the mouse to drag the checkbox control to wherever we like.

Any time we add a control to the program we need to set or change its properties. Here are some of the checkbox properties we might consider setting or changing.

Name .. To make writing the source code less confusing let's change the name of the checkbox control to (ChkBoxTwice). As our Hello program grows in size it is a good idea to have the name of each control reflect its type, in this case checkbox, and what it does, display Hello twice.

CheckState .. We can use this property to indicate that when the program is run we want the checkbox to already be checked. For this example, let's leave the check state property unchecked.

Text .. We can use this property to specify the text that is displayed beside the checkbox. Let's change the text property to (Display twice).

We have now added a checkbox control to our program and set its properties. Similar to the button control, the next step is creating the source code that will respond to the user checking or unchecking the checkbox. The procedure for adding the source code to handle the checkbox control is similar to the procedure for coding the button control.

CHECKBOX CONTROL SOURCE CODE

If necessary, switch from the form design frame back to the code frame by clicking the (Form1.vb) tab.

As with the source code for the button control, the first thing we have to do is decide where to put the code. We want the code for the checkbox control to be executed whenever the user checks or unchecks the checkbox. In other words, when the control's checked status changes.

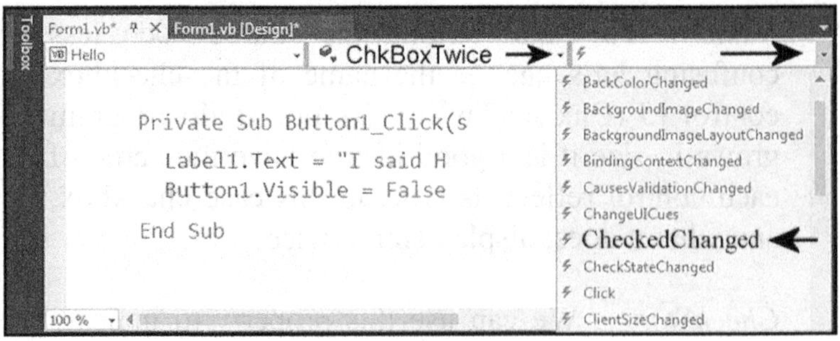

To create the section in our program where we can put the source code to handle the checkbox control we can do the following.

1 .. Click the little black triangle on the right side of the middle box to drop down the list of controls and then select the (ChkBoxTwice) control.

2 .. Click the little black triangle in the box on the right to drop down the list of events and select the (CheckedChanged) event.

Once we select the (Checked-Changed) event, visual studio will create a little section of code called (*Private Sub ChkBoxTwice-CheckedChanged*). This is where we put the source code to respond to the user checking or unchecking the checkbox control.

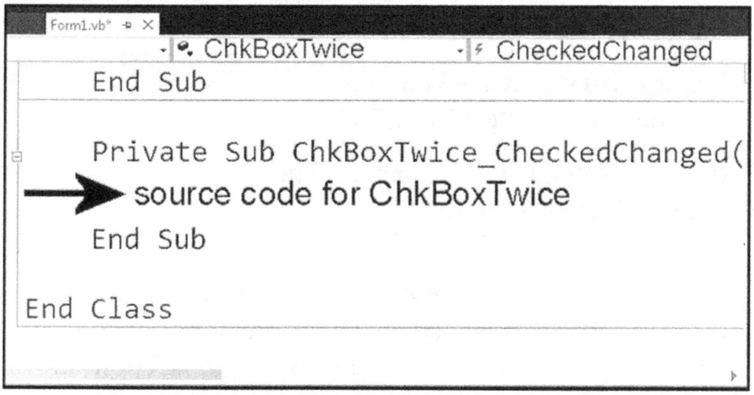

The source code for the ChkBoxTwice control is a little different than the code we used for the button control. There is only one thing the user can do to the button control, click it. There are two things the user can do to the checkbox control, check it or uncheck it.

> If the user checks the ChkBoxTwice control, then we want the program to display (Hello Hello) in the label control.
>
> If the user unchecks the ChkBoxTwice control, then we want the program to display (Hello) in the label control.
>
> To keep the Button control from interfering with the actions performed by the checkbox, let's disable the Button1 control.

For the ChkBoxTwice control we need two lines of source code, and to disable the Button1 control we need one line of source code. The three lines of code that do this are

Button1.Visible = False
If ChkBoxTwice.Checked Then _ Label1.Text = "Hello Hello"
If Not ChkBoxTwice.Checked Then _ Label1.Text = "Hello"

The tricky part is that we need to disable the button control before the program is loaded. Therefore, the code to disable Button1 need to be in the Form1-Load section of the program. The code for the checkboxes goes in the ChkBoxTwice-CheckedChanged section. After we add the three lines of code our program should look like this.

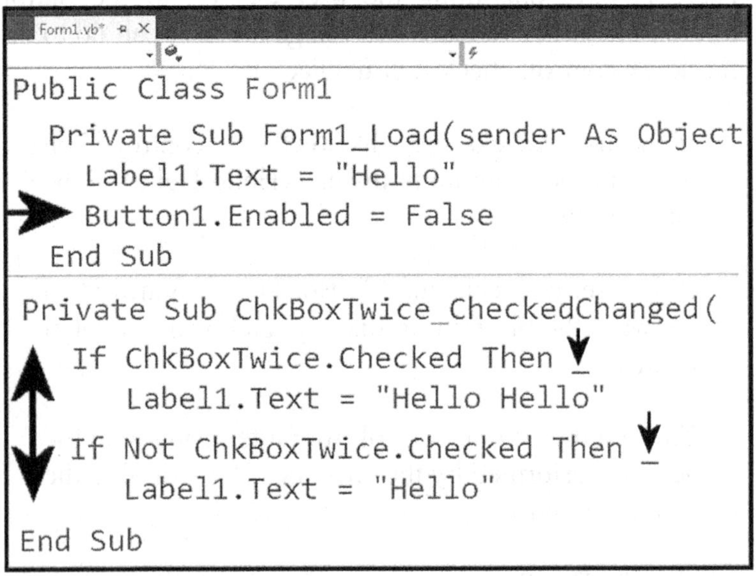

Notice that for the button control there is no disable property, just an enable property that we set to either true or false.

Another thing to notice with this code is how we can break up a long statement into multiple lines by ending each line with an underscore _.

The code for the checkbox control is a new type of statement called an (IF) statement. We will learn more about the IF statement later. The basic structures of the IF statement are

If something   Then something else
If not something   Then something else

If we test our enhanced Hello program by clicking the Start icon ▶ in the toolbar we should get.

<table>
<tr><th>ChkBoxTwice unchecked</th><th>ChkBoxTwice checked</th></tr>
<tr><td>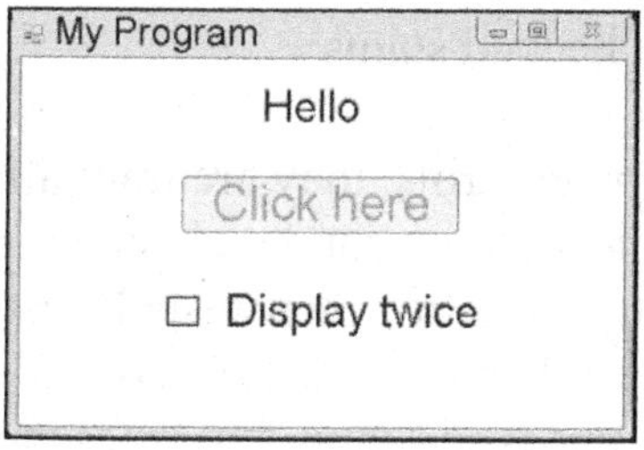
</td><td>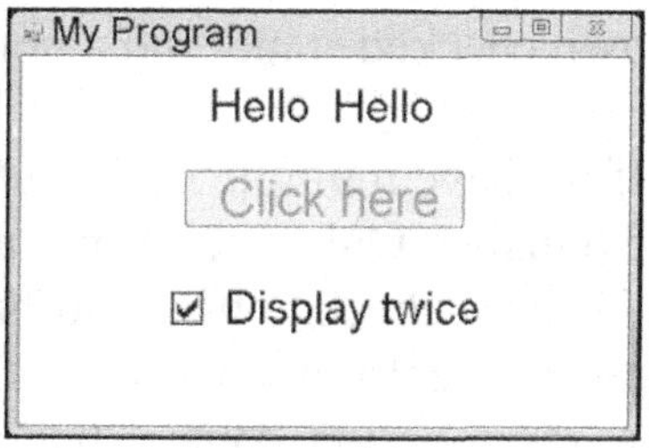
</td></tr>
</table>

Notice that the button control is visible, but nothing happens when we try to click it, it is disabled.

Now that the display-twice checkbox control seems to be working let's look at a control that is similar but different, a radio-button control. Similar to the checkbox control, the purpose of a radio-button control is to have the program do something whenever the user checks or unchecks the radio-button. To see the difference between checkbox controls and radio-button controls consider the following program.

If we have multiple checkbox controls, each one is independent of the other. None, some, or all of the checkboxes can be checked. Each checkbox control has its own checked status and a not-checked status.

If we have multiple radio-button controls, they are mutually exclusive. Only one of the radio-buttons can be checked. If the user checks one radio-button control then visual basic automatically unchecks all the other radio-button controls. A radio-button control has a checked status but does not have a not-checked status.

For our next version of the Hello program, let's have the checkboxes and radio-buttons do the following.

> The two checkboxes are there for demo purposes only, we won't be adding any source code for them. Neither, one, or both of the checkboxes can be checked.

If the user checks the black radio-button, then we want the program to display Hello in black letters.

If the user checks the red radio-button, then we want the program to display Hello in red letters.

We use radio-buttons for the color of the word Hello because the color can be black or red but not both.

RADIO BUTTON CONTROL

Hopefully, by now, we have learned how to add controls to the program.

1 .. Go to the form design frame by clicking the (Form1.vb Design) tab.

2 .. Click the word (Toolbox) and then the word (Common Controls).

3 .. Use the mouse to drag two (CheckBox) controls and two (RadioButton) controls to the form design frame.

For the two checkbox controls, the only property we need to set is the Text property. For CheckBox1 let's set the Text property to (*Run program on weekdays*). And for CheckBox2 let's set the Text property to (*Run program on weekends*).

Here are some of the radio-button properties we might consider setting or changing.

Name .. Let's change the Name of RadioButton1 to (RadButBlack) and the Name of RadioButton2 to (RadButRed).

Checked .. We can use this property to indicate that when the program is run we want this radio-button to already be checked. For this example, let's set the checked property of (RadButBlack) to (True).

Text .. We can use this property to specify the text that is displayed beside the radio-button. Let's change the Text property of RadButBlack to (Black) and the Text property of RadButRed to (Red).

While we are in the process of adding controls let's remove the display-twice checkbox we added in the previous example. To remove a control from the form design frame all we have to do is select the control and hit the (Delete) key. Once the control is removed from the form design frame we have to go to the code frame and delete the source code for the control, including the (Private Sub) and (End Sub) statements. With regards to deleting, copying, pasting, and searching the visual studio IDE works the same way as a word processing program.

After adding the four controls the next step is to create the source code for the two radio-button controls.

RADIO BUTTON CONTROL SOURCE CODE

As with the other controls, the first step in adding source code is to decide where to put the source code. We want the source code for a radio-button control to be executed whenever the user checks the radio-button. In other words, when the control's checked status changes.

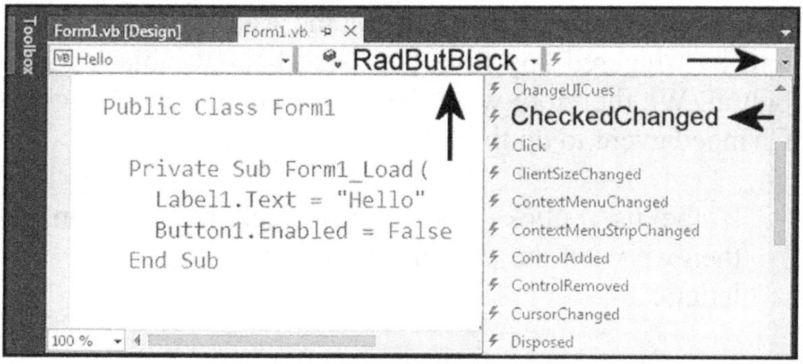

Let's put the source code for the black radio-button in the (Checked-Changed) event of the (RadButBlack) control.

1 .. In the middle box, we want to select the (RadButBlack) control.

2 .. In the box on the right, we want to select the (CheckedChanged) event.

Selecting the Checked-Changed event will create the (RadButBlack-CheckedChanged) subroutine. This is where we put the source code to respond to the user checking the RadButBlack control.

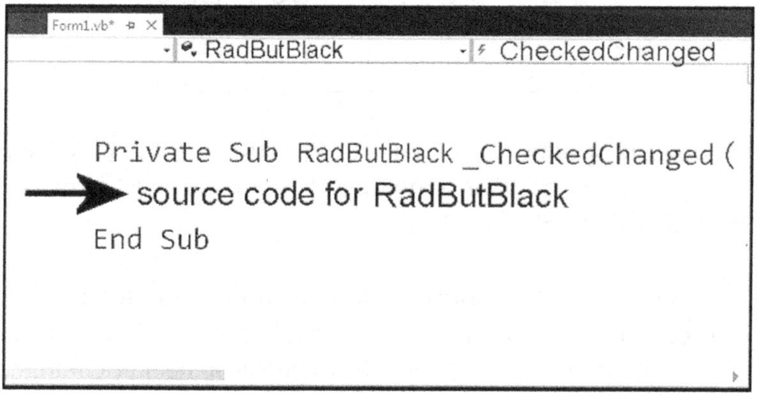

The Checked-Changed event for the RadButBlack control will be triggered any time the user clicks the black radio-button. We therefore want the source code in the Checked-Changed event to do the following.

> If the user clicks the RadButBlack radio-button, then we want the program to display Hello in black letters.

For the RadButBlack-CheckedChanged subroutine, we therefore need the following line of source code.

```
If RadButBlack.Checked Then _
   Label1.ForeColor = Color.Black
```

After we add this line of code to the RadButBlack-CheckedChanged event our program should look like this.

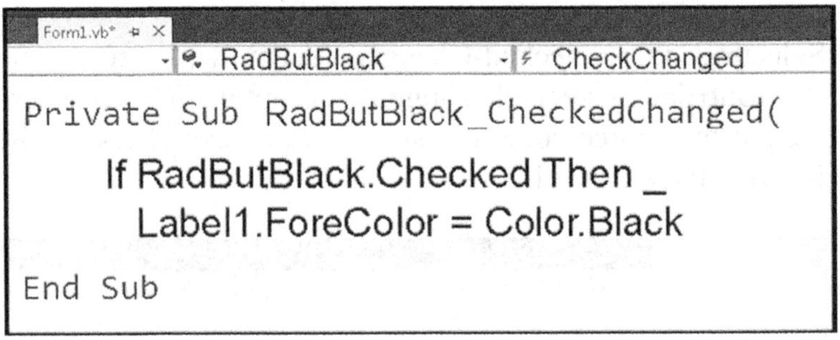

Notice the syntax for specifying the color of whatever text is in the label control. Once again we used the (property) period (value) syntax.

We now need to follow a similar procedure to add the source code to handle the red radio-button. That source code needs to be in the RadButRed-CheckedChanged subroutine. When we are finished, our program should look like this.

```
Private Sub RadButBlack_CheckedChanged(
    If RadButBlack.Checked Then _
      Label1.ForeColor = Color.Black
End Sub
```

```
Private Sub RadButRed_CheckedChanged(
    If RadButRed.Checked Then _
      Label1.ForeColor = Color.Red
End Sub
```

If we test our new program by clicking the Start icon ► in the toolbar we should get.

RadButBlack checked	RadButRed checked

Notice that nothing happens when we check or uncheck the checkbox controls. We did not add any source code for the checkboxes. They are there to show that checkbox controls are independent. None, one, or all of the checkboxes can be checked.

So much to do, so little time. According to the Toolbox, there are about 996 more controls to look at. And after that, we can go on the internet and buy controls that other programmers have written. In reality, most large program can be written using less than 20 different types of controls.

In the next chapter, we will look at some of the other controls.

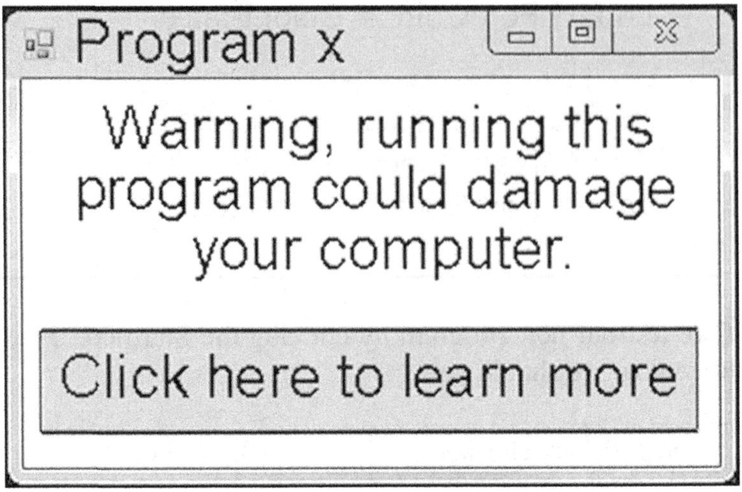

==

Chapter 4
MORE CONTROLS

In the previous chapter, we learned how to use the label control, the button control, the checkbox control, and the radio button control. In this chapter, we will learn about some more controls. Like the previous controls, we will add the new controls to our program, set their properties, and then add source code that the program will execute when the controls are triggered.

There are hundreds of controls, and more can be acquired from the internet, but we only need to look at a few of them. The 65,000-line computer program that I wrote for ham radio operators, called MicroLog, uses no more than 20 different types of controls. A free website version of MicroLog can be downloaded from my website (www.wa0h.com). The 0 in wa0h is the number zero.

Since this is a new chapter, let's bring up the visual studio Start Page and create a new program called (Controls).

1 .. If the Hello program is still open then save the Hello program. After saving the Hello program click the word (File) in the menu bar and then select (Close Project) or (Close Solution). The Get Started screen should now be open.

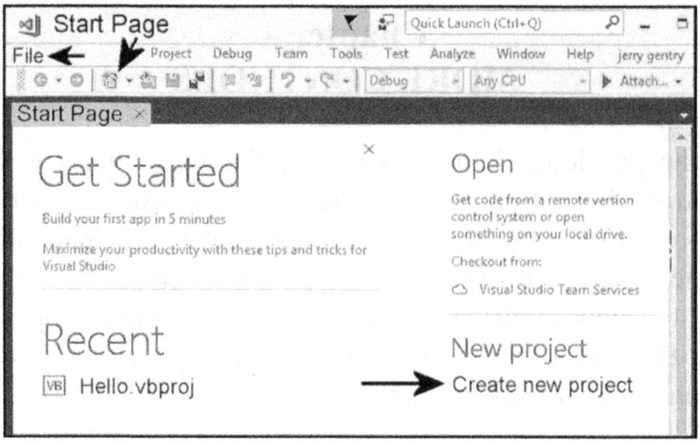

2 .. On the Get Started screen, click (Create new project) to start a new program. You can also start a new program by clicking the word (File) in the menu bar and then selecting (New Project). A third way to start a new program is by clicking the New Project icon in the toolbar.

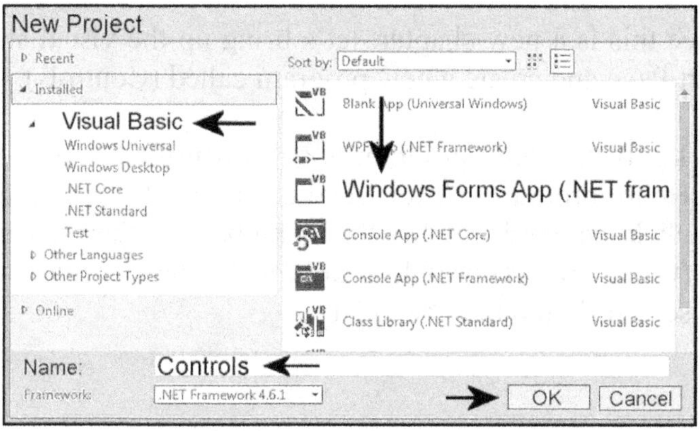

3 .. On the left side of the New Projects screen select (Visual Basic). On the right side of the New Projects screen select (Windows Forms App). For the Name of the program enter (Controls). The last step is to click (OK).

We should now be in the form design frame where we can design our new program. Let's start by changing the name in the program's title bar to (Controls).

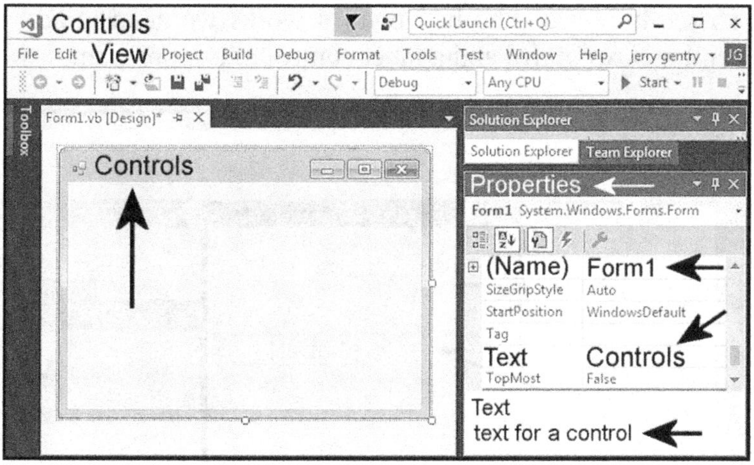

1 .. Make sure we are in the form design frame by clicking the tab (Form1.vb Design).

2 .. Make sure the Properties frame is visible.

3 .. Select the Form control and then set the (Text) property to the word (Controls).

We can now start adding controls to our new program. One control is not more important than another control so let's just add them in the order they are listed in the Common Controls section of the toolbox frame. As for the controls we skip over, it is easy to see what they do by searching the internet. For our first control let's add a combo-box control to our program.

COMBO BOX CONTROL

A combo-box control is used to display a drop-down list of various items allowing the user to select one of the items. To see how a combo-box control works we need to add a combo-box control and a label control to our program.

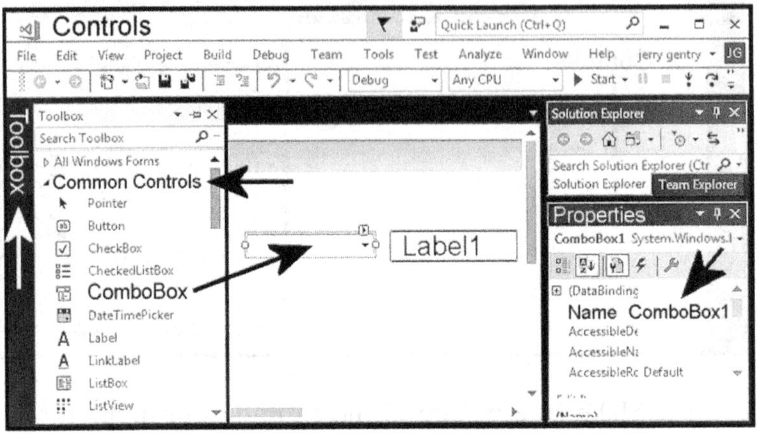

As a refresher, to add these controls we do the following.

1 .. Click the word (Toolbox) and then the words (Common Controls).

2 .. Use the mouse to drag a (ComboBox) control and a (Label) control to the form design frame.

After adding a control, the next step is setting or changing the properties of the control. For the combo-box let's change the following properties.

DropDownStyle .. This property changes the way the combo-box control works. We need to set the DropDownStyle property to (DropDownList).

Items .. This property allows us to enter a list of items in the combo-box. To enter items in the combo-box we do the following.

1 .. Select the combo-box control.

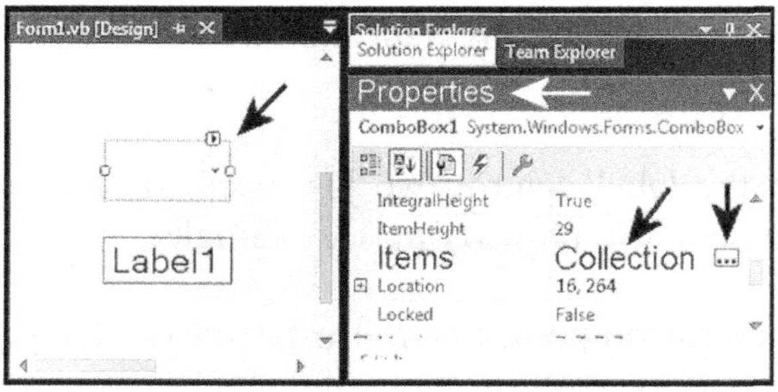

2 .. In the properties frame, click the word (Collection) on the (Items) property line and then click the three dots at the end of the line. This will bring up the String Collection Editor window.

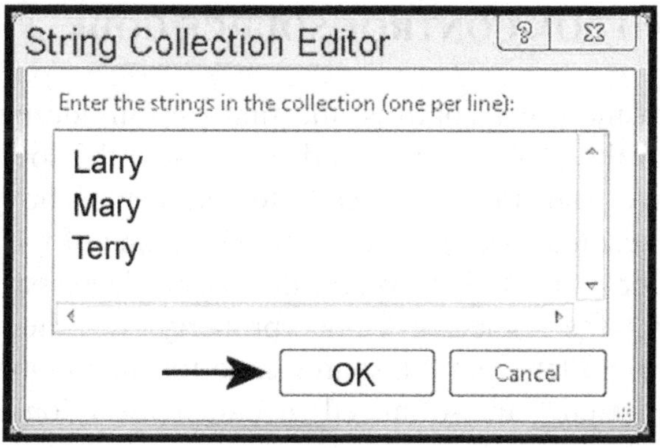

3 .. For the items in the combo-box let's enter Larry, Mary, and Terry. Enter one item per line. Do not hit the Enter key after entering the last item, just click (OK).

When the program returns to the form design frame there may not be any indication that the items were added.

For the label control, we just need to change the (BorderStyle) property to (FixedSingle).

Most control properties can also be set or changed using source code. We will see more of that in later chapters.

After setting the properties of the two controls the next step is to create the source code for the controls. We want the program to allow the user to select one of the names in the drop-down combo-box and then display that name in the label box.

COMBO BOX CONTROL SOURCE CODE

As with the other controls, the first step in adding source code for the combo-box is to decide where the source code goes. We want the source code for the combo-box control to be executed whenever the user selects one of the choices in the drop-down list. When the user selects one of the choices, the Selected-Value property of the control changes. So let's put the source code for the combo-box in the (Selected-Value-Changed) event of the (ComboBox1) control.

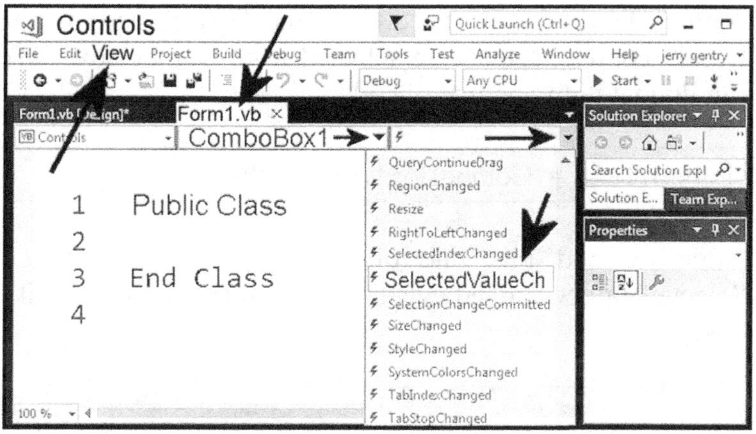

To create the Selected-Value-Changed section of code we can do the following.

1 .. Switch to the code frame by clicking the word (View) in the menu bar and then selecting (Code), or by clicking the (Form1.vb) tab.

2 .. In the middle box, above where we write source code, click the black triangle on the right side of the box to drop down the list of controls and then select the (ComboBox1) control.

3 .. In the box on the right, drop down the list of events and select the (SelectedValueChanged) event.

Selecting the (Selected-Value-Changed) event will create the (ComboBox1-SelectedValueChanged) subroutine where we can put the source code to respond to the user selecting one of the names in the drop-down list of names.

We want the program to take the name the user selects from the drop-down combo-box and display it in the label control. To do this we need to set the Text property of the Label1 control to the item selected from ComboBox1. We can do that with one line of code.

```
Label1.Text = ComboBox1.SelectedItem
```

After we add this line of code to the ComboBox1-SelectedValueChanged event, our program should look like this.

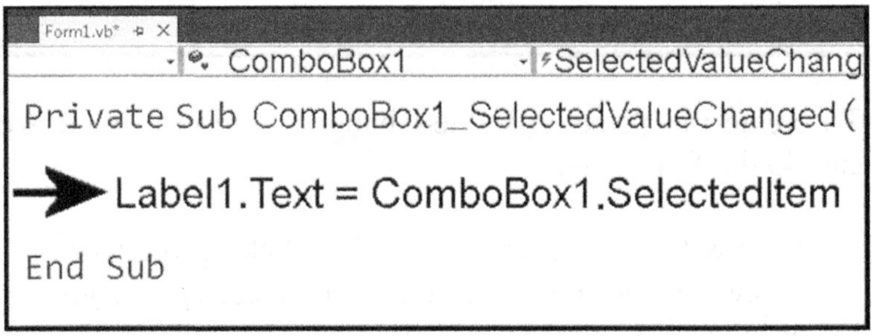

Notice that once again we are using the (Control) period (property) syntax. Before we test our new Controls program we should save it.

1 .. Click the word (File) in the menu bar and then select (Save All).

2 .. On the Save Project screen enter the program name, (Controls), and the location of where we want to save the program, (C:\My-Programs).

3 .. Uncheck the (Create directory) checkbox.

4 .. Click the (Save) button.

Our Controls program is now saved in folder (C:\My-Programs\Controls). The only thing left to do is test our new program by clicking the Start icon ▶ in the toolbar.

before selection	after selection
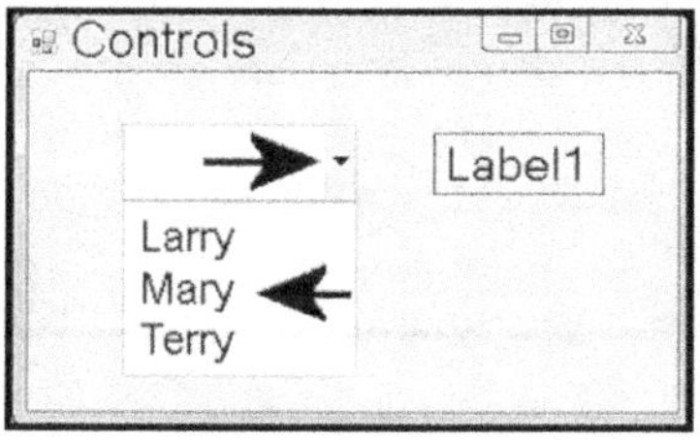	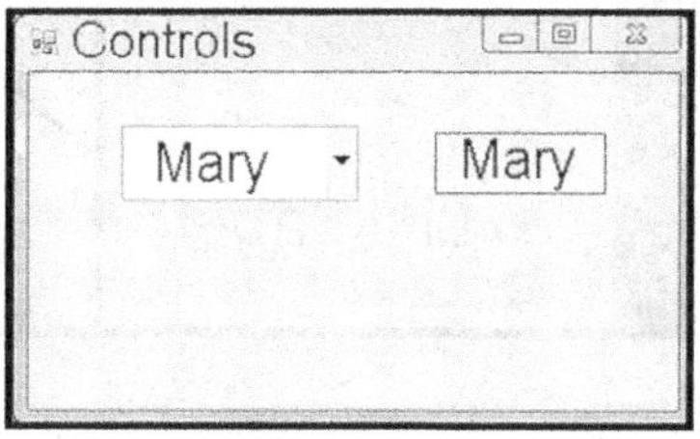

To select a name from the combo-box control we click the black triangle on the right side of the combo-box and then click one of the names in the box. Once we select a name, that name is displayed in the label control.

We will learn more about what we can do with these controls when we get to the chapters on coding. For now, let's look at our next control, the LinkLabel control.

LINK LABEL CONTROL

We have made several references to using the internet. It would be nice if our program could access the internet, and it can if we add a link-label control to the program.

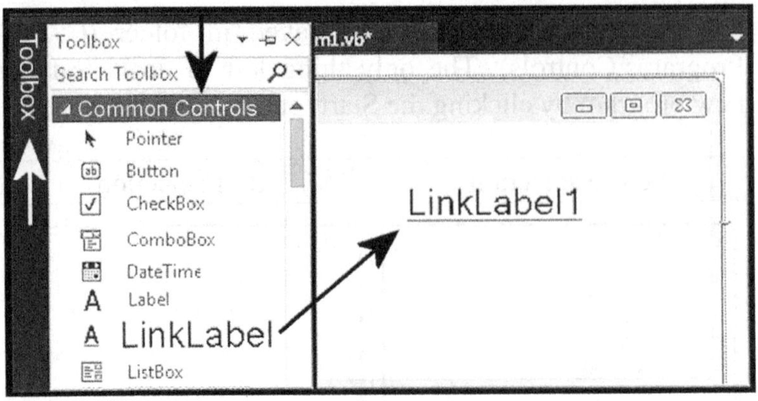

Adding the link-label control to the program is like adding any other control, just use the mouse to drag the word LinkLabel from the toolbox to the form design frame.

After adding the link-label control we need to set or change the following properties.

> *Text* .. We can use this property to specify the words that appear when the program is run. Let's change (LinkLabel1) to (access Google website).
>
> *LinkArea* .. The normal way to indicate that some words are a link to the internet is to underline the words. By default, all the words in the control are underlined. Let's change that so that just the word Google is underlined. In the words (access Google website), the (G) in Google is the 7th character. We want it and the next 6 characters underlined so we need to set the (LinkArea) property to (7,6).

Before you call me to inform me that the (G) in (access Google website) is the 8th character, let me explain. We humans start counting with the number 1. But computers, which are smarter than humans, start counting with the number zero. So, any time we want the program to reference some position we have to remember that, to the computer, the 1st position is position zero.

After setting the properties of the link-label control the next step is to create the source code for the control. We want the program to access the Google website anytime the user clicks the link word (Google).

LINK-LABEL CONTROL SOURCE CODE

We want the source code for the link-label control to be executed whenever the link word Google is clicked so we need to put the source code in the (Link-Clicked) event of the (LinkLabel1) control.

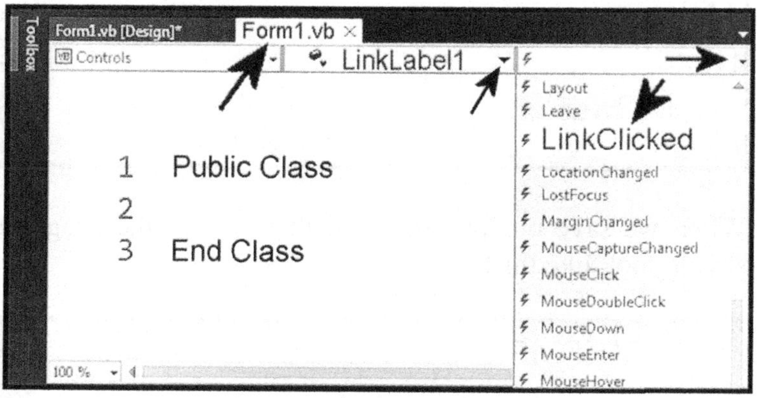

To create the Link-Clicked section of code we switch to the (Form1.vb) tab, select the (LinkLabel1) control from the middle box, and select the (LinkClicked) event from the box on the right.

All we need to do to access the internet, assuming we have an internet connection, is specify the address of the website we want to go to.

Since the address of the Google website is (www.google.com), one line of code in the Link-Clicked section of code will make the program work.

```
Process.Start ("www.google.com")
```

After we add this line of code to the LinkLabel1-LinkClicked section our program should look like this.

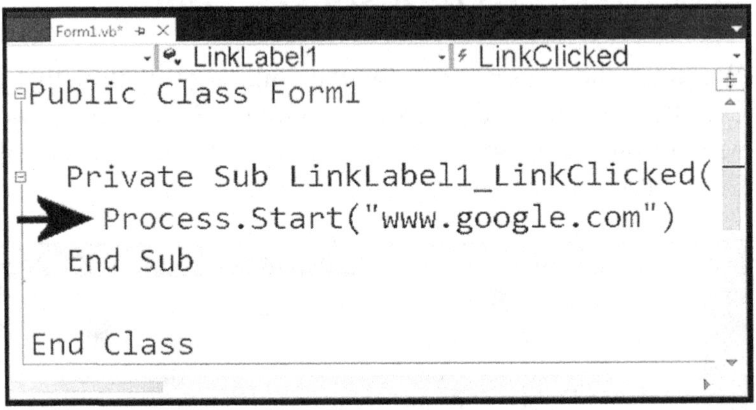

When we save our program and then test it, the program should look like this.

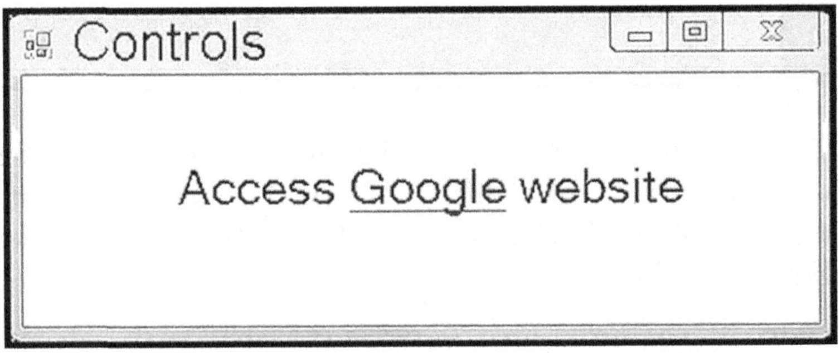

When we click the word in the link that is underlined, in this case Google, the Google website will open. It should be noted that the website and the program are two independent windows. We can close either the Google webpage or our program without affecting the other window. Later, if my arthritic hands hold out, we will learn how to have the webpage, or an image from the website, open inside our program.

The combo-box control we had earlier allowed us to select a name from a list of names. Our next control expands on that ability. Suppose we want to select a record from a table of data.

Name	Age	Family	Weight	Height	Birthday
Larry	25	Yes	170	5'10"	Jan 1
Mary	35	No	140	5'4"	July 15
Terry	45	???	150	5'8"	Dec 31

To select a record from a table we can use either a list-box control or a list-view control.

LIST-BOX AND LIST-VIEW CONTROLS

The list-view control is similar to the list-box control except it is more powerful. For this reason, let's just look at the list-view control. It may seem like this exercise takes forever but after you have added a couple of list-view controls to a program the process goes quickly. Let's start by adding a list-view control and two additional label controls to our program.

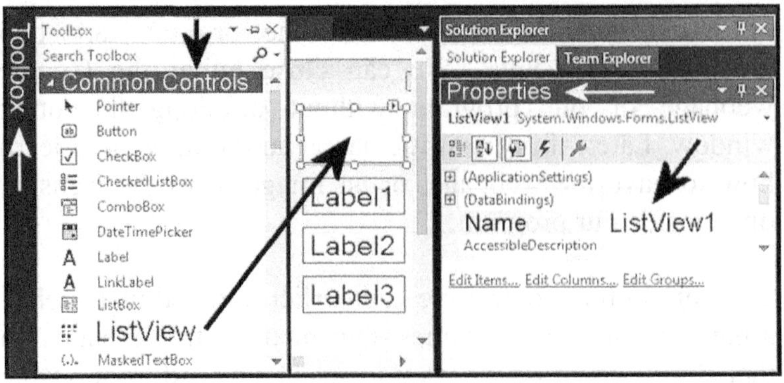

After adding the list-view and label controls we need to set or change some of their properties. For the two new label controls let's change the (BorderStyle) property to (FixedSingle). For the list-view control, there are several properties we need to change.

> *View* .. This property determines how the list-view control looks and works. We need to change the View property to (Details).
>
> *FullRowSelect* .. Set this property to (True). When the user selects a row, the whole row will be highlighted.
>
> *GridLines* .. Set this property to (True).

It takes several steps to add data records to the list-view table. For most programs adding data records is done using source code. To add data records during the design phase we have to create the (columns) and then create the data (items) or records.

To create the columns, we put values into the Columns property of the list-view control. This process takes several steps. For simplicity, let's make our list-view control have just three columns, Name, Age, and Family-status. To create the columns, we do the following.

1 .. Select the list-view control.

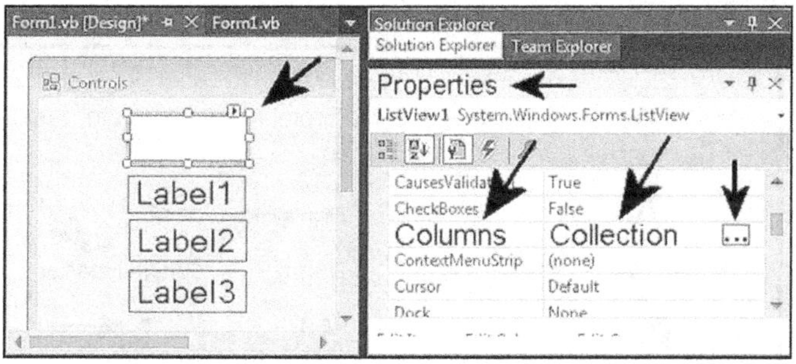

2 .. In the properties frame, click the word (Collection) on the (Columns) property line and then click the three dots at the end of the line. This will bring up the Column-Header Collection Editor window.

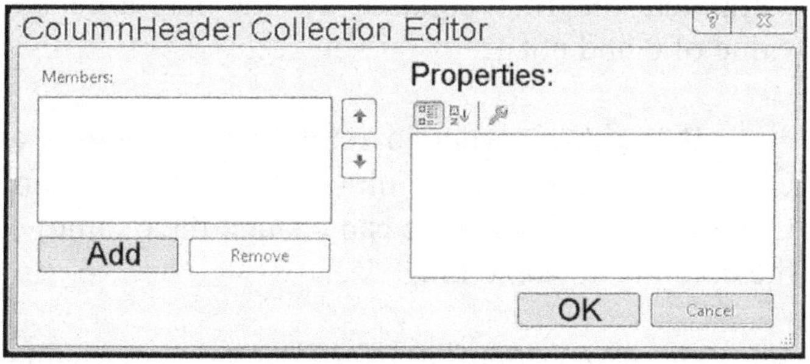

3 .. Add each column to the list-view control by doing steps (3a) through (3d). Do not click the (OK) button until all three columns have been added.

--- Add a column ---------------------------------------

3a .. Click the (Add) button. This will expand the properties frame on the right side of the Column-Header Collection Editor.

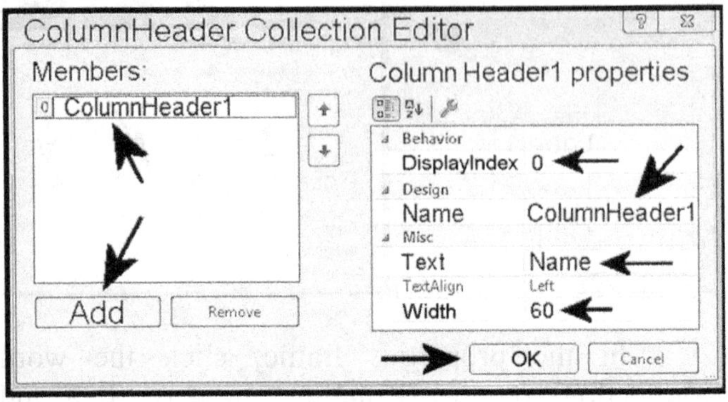

Remember what we said earlier about how a computer counts, (0,1,2...) instead of (1,2,3...)? The (DisplayIndex) line on the right says that, to the computer, the first column we add has an index value of 0 and not 1.

3b .. If we don't want to refer to the columns as ColumnHeader1, ColumnHeader2, and ColumnHeader3, then we can change the (Name) of the columns to something else.

3c .. The (Text) field is where we enter the names we want displayed in the column headers when the program is running. Let's display (Name) for column 1, (Age) for column 2, and (Family) for column 3.

3d .. For the (Width) field, let's make the width of the Name field 80, the width of the Age field 60, and the width of the Family field 100. We may need to revise these numbers once we test the program with some actual data.

--- End of - Add a column -----------------------------

When all columns have been added then we can click the (OK) button. Our form design frame should now look something like this.

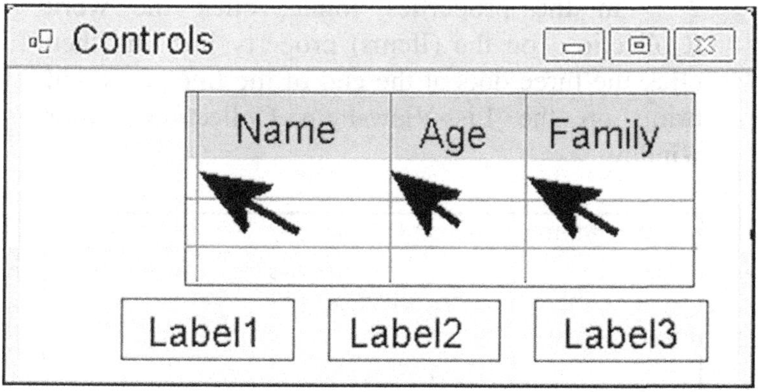

If nothing appears in the column headers then use the mouse to drag the faint vertical lines to the right. These lines change the width of the columns. Also, make sure the View property is set to Details.

Now that we have the columns let's fill in the list-view table with some records. To enter name-age-family records we do the following.

1 .. Select the list-view control.

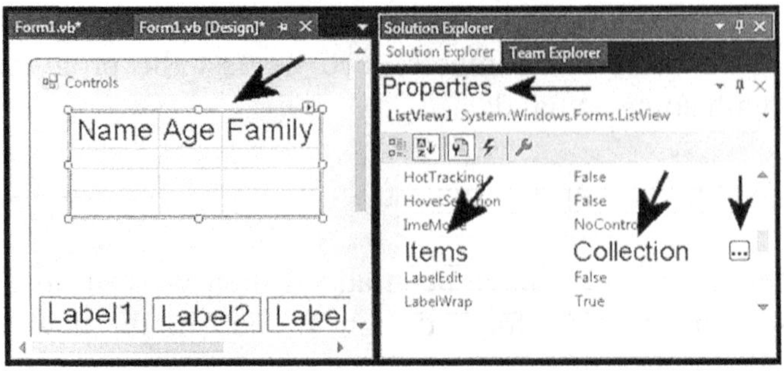

2 .. In the properties frame, click the word (Collection) on the (Items) property line and then click the three dots at the end of the line. This will bring up the List-View-Item Collection Editor window.

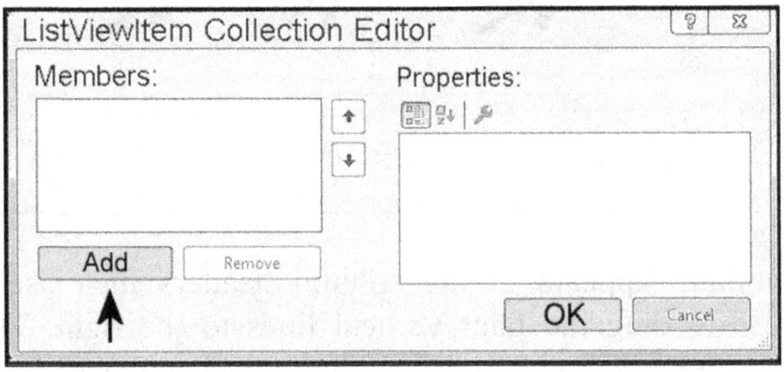

=== Add a (name-age-family) record ==========

To add each record to our list-view table we have to first add the Name, which is called an (Item). Then we add the Age and Family-status, which are called (Sub-Items). To add each name-age-family record we do steps 3 through 7.

--- Add the Name --

3 .. Click the (Add) button to add the Name of the person. This will expand the properties frame of the ListViewItem Collection Editor.

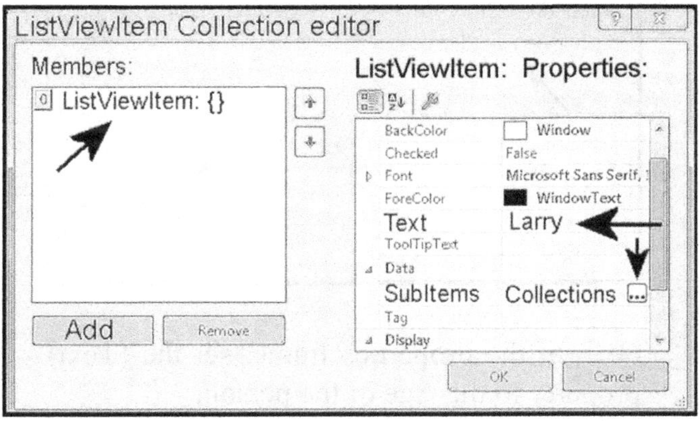

4 .. In the properties frame, set the (Text) property to the Name of the person. We now have to enter the Age and Family-status of this person.

5 .. Click the word (Collection) on the (SubItems) line and then click the three dots at the end of the line. This will bring up a (List-View-SubItem) window where we can enter the Age of the person and the Family-status of the person.

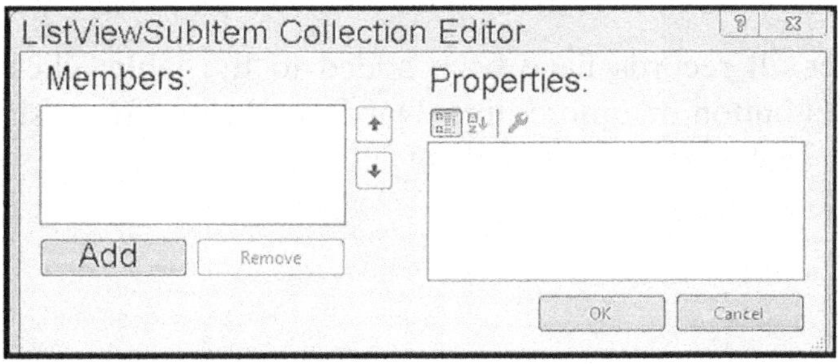

--- Add the Age and Family-status -----------

6a .. Click the (Add) button. This will bring up a window where we can add the Age.

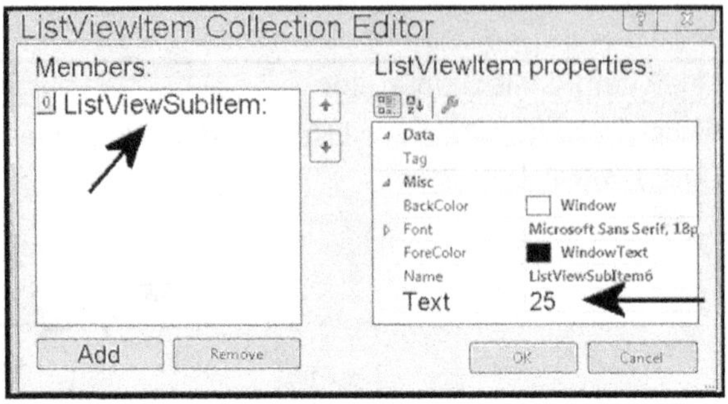

6b .. In the properties frame, set the (Text) property to the Age of the person.

6c .. Repeat steps 6a and 6b to add the Family-status.

-- End of add Age and Family-status ---------

7 .. After the Name, Age, and Family-status values have been added, click the (OK) button to add the record to the table.

=== End of add a record =========

After all records have been added to the table, click the (OK) button one more time. Our form design frame should now look something like this.

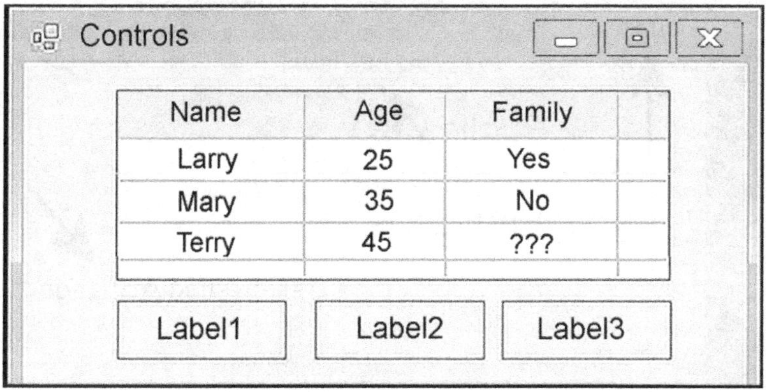

If we are going to create a big table with lots of records, then it will be much easier to create the table using source code. After creating the list-view control the next step is to create the source code for the control. We want the program to allow the user to select one of the records in the table and then display the name, age, and family-status of the selected record in the label boxes.

LISTVIEW CONTROL SOURCE CODE

As to where to put the source code for the list-view control, we want the program to respond whenever the user selects one of the records in the table. To do this we can put the source code for the list-view control in the (Selected-Index-Changed) event of the (ListView1) control.

You may wonder why we used the Selected-Value-Changed event for the combo-box control but the Selected-Index-Changed event for the list-view control. The answer is probably because these controls were developed at different times by different people.

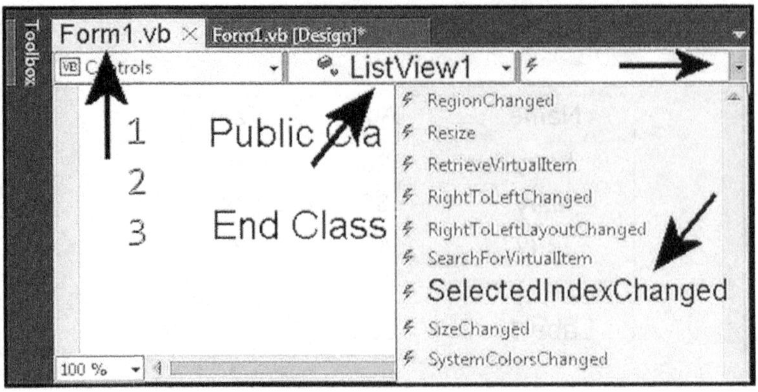

To create the Selected-Index-Changed section of code we switch to the (Form1.vb) tab, select the (ListView1) control for the middle box, and select the (Selected-Index-Changed) event for the box on the right.

We want the program to display the name, age, and family-status of the record selected by the user. To do this we need to set the Text property of the labels to the values selected from the table. We can do this with three lines of code.

```
Label1.Text = ListView1.SelectedItems.Item(0).Text

Label2.Text = _
  ListView1.SelectedItems(0).SubItems(1).Text

Label3.Text = _
  ListView1.SelectedItems(0).SubItems(2).Text
```

After we add these three lines of code to the (ListView1-SelectedIndexChanged) section of our program the subroutine should look like this.

```
Private Sub ListView1_SelectedIndexChanged (
  Label1.Text = ListView1.SelectedItems.Item(0).Text
  Label2.Text = ListView1.SelectedItems(0).SubItems(1).Text
  Label3.Text = ListView1.SelectedItems(0).SubItems(2).Text
End Sub
```

Sometimes learning how to write a line of source code that will do a certain thing is like learning how to spell a word like photo. You just have to memorize that it is photo and not foto. This is why I make cheat sheets of "*To do this, use this line of code.*".

We are now ready to save our program and then test it by clicking the word Start in the toolbar.

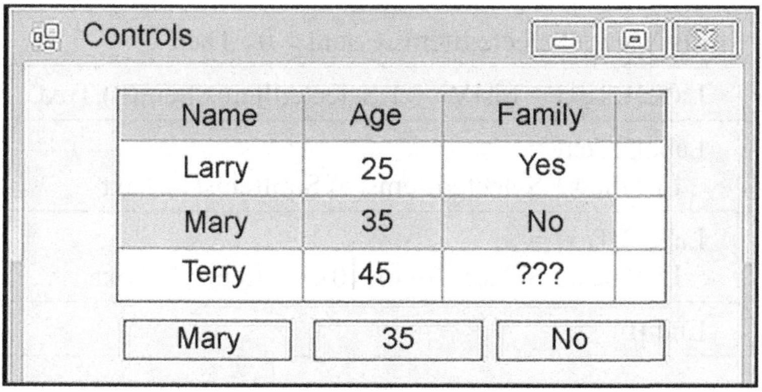

If we select the Mary record the program responds by displaying the data for Mary in the labels. Now, select either the Larry record or the Terry record. A little window opens up in our source code frame that says something like

```
System.ArgumentOutOfRangeException:
'InvalidArgument=Value of '0' is not valid for 'index'.
Parameter name: index'
```

I lied again. It appears that it takes more than three lines of code. I forgot that there is a little quirk regarding list-view controls. To help find the bug we can search the internet.

> If we do an internet search for "*visual basic System.ArgumentOutOfRangeException: InvalidArgument=Value of 0 is not valid for index*", we can find a website that tells us we need to add an extra line of code for listview controls.

First, we need to shut down the test by clicking the Stop icon ■ in the toolbar.

Next, we need to put our three lines of code inside an (IF) statement. The symbol > means greater than.

If ListView1.SelectedItems.Count > 0 Then
Label1.Text = ListView1.SelectedItems.Item(0).Text
Label2.Text = _ ListView1.SelectedItems(0).SubItems(1).Text
Label3.Text = _ ListView1.SelectedItems (0).SubItems(2).Text
End If

Our program should now look like this.

```
Form1.vb*          Form1          InitializeComponent
Private Sub ListView1_SelectedIndexChanged (
    If ListView1.SelectedItems.Count > 0 Then
        Label1.Text = ListView1.SelectedItems.Item(0).Text
        Label2.Text = ListView1.SelectedItems(0).SubItems(1).Text
        Label3.Text = ListView1.SelectedItems(0).SubItems(2).Text
    End If
End Sub
```

Earlier we had an (IF) statement of the form

```
IF something   THEN do this
```

If there are several statements that need to be conditionally done then the form of the (IF) statement is

```
IF something THEN
    do this
    and this
    END IF
```

If we now test our program it should work. Fortunately, these quirks don't occur that often in visual basic. Our next control is a little easier to work with

MONTH-CALENDAR CONTROL

A month-calendar control allows the user to select a date from a calendar. Let's start by adding a month-calendar control to our program. We can use the same Label1 control that we used in the previous exercises.

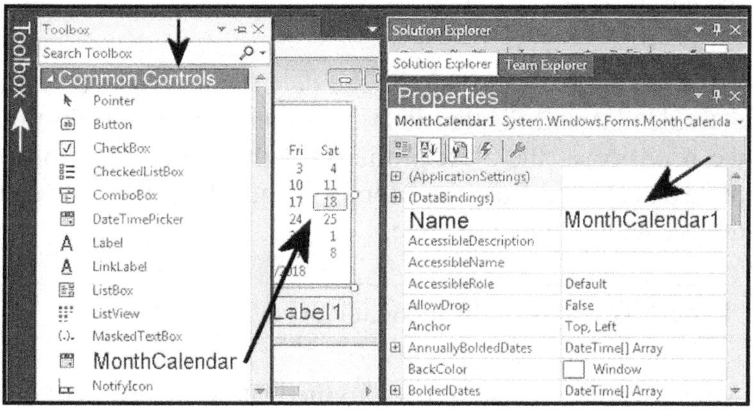

After adding the month-calendar control we have the option of setting or changing its properties. For this example, we don't need to change any of the properties.

MONTH-CALENDAR CONTROL SOURCE CODE

The next step is to create the source code for the control. We want the program to allow the user to select a date from the calendar and then display that date in the label box. When the user selects a date, the Date-Selected value assigned to the control changes, so we need to put the source code in the (Date-Selected) event of the (MonthCalendar1) control.

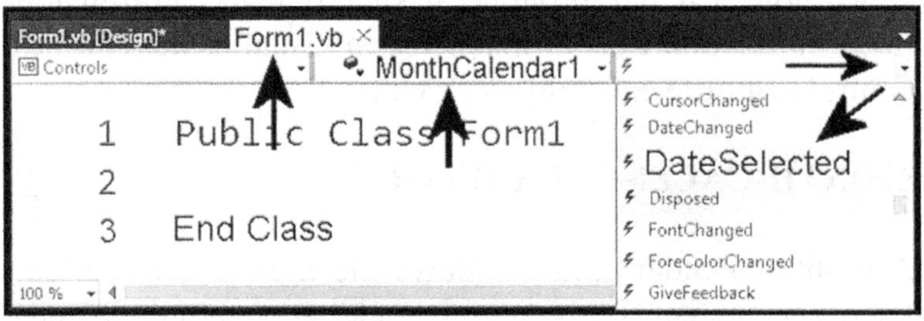

To create the Date-Selected section of code we select the (MonthCalendar1) control from the middle box and the (DateSelected) event from the box on the right.

We want the program to take the date the user selects from the calendar and display it in the label control. To do this we need to set the Text property of the Label1 control to the date selected from the MonthCalendar1 control. We can do this with one line of code.

```
Label1.Text = MonthCalendar1.SelectionStart
```

After we add this line of code to the DateSelected event our program should look like this.

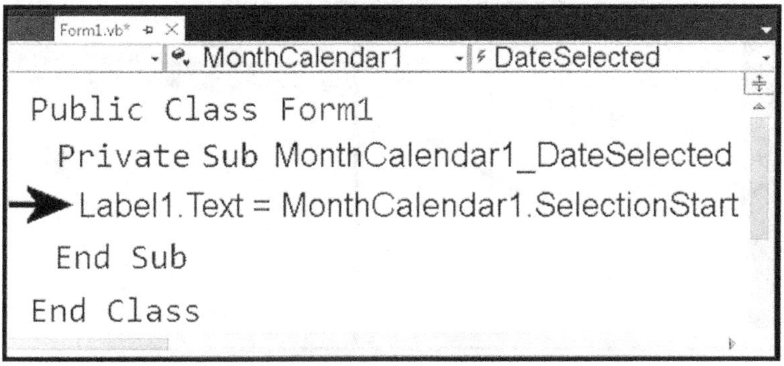

We are now ready to save our program and then test it. If we select the date August 19th, then 8/19/2018 will appear in the label control.

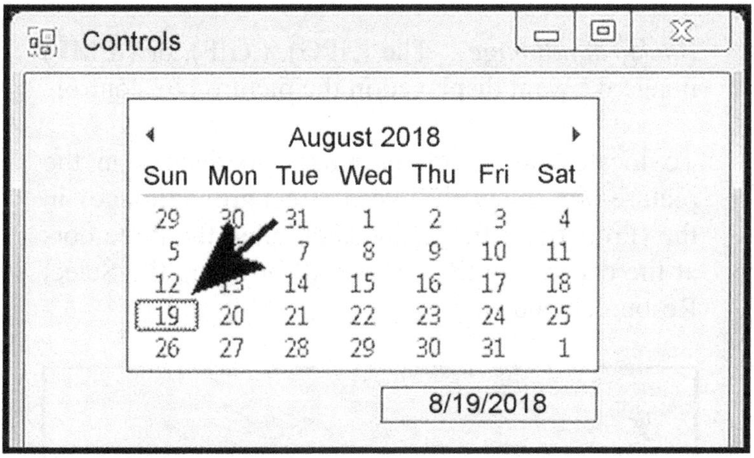

Suppose we want to display a picture inside our program. Our next control will let us do that.

PICTURE BOX CONTROL

A picture-box control is a frame inside our program where we can insert a picture. Let's start by adding a picture-box control to our program.

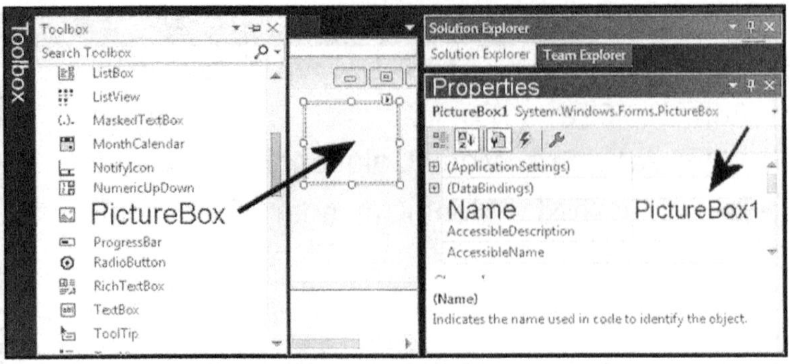

After adding the picture-box control we need to set or change its properties.

BorderStyle .. Change to (FixedSingle).

BackgroundImage .. The (.JPG), (.GIF), or (.BMP) image we want displayed in the picture-box control.

To locate and select the image to display in the picture-box, click the word (BackgroundImage) in the (Properties) frame and then click the three dots at the end of the line. This will bring up the Select Resource window.

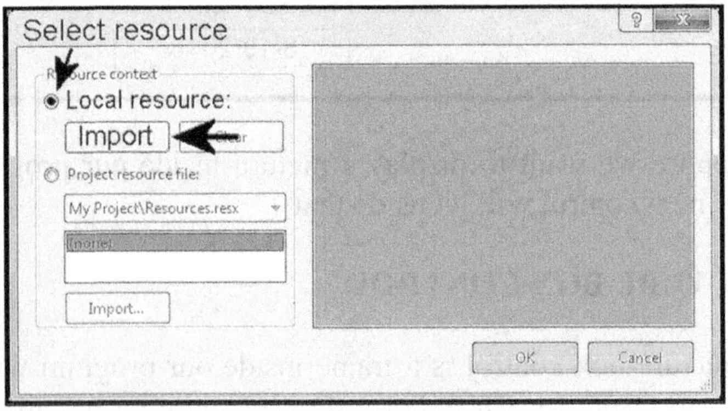

Click the (Local resource) radio-button and then click the (Import) button. This will bring up a window that will allow us to locate and open the image we want to display in the picture-box control.

Once we select the image that we want to display in our program click the (OPEN) button. Then, on the next screen click the (OK) button.

BackgroundImageLayout .. Set this property to (Stretch) so the image will fit inside the picture-box control.

For the picture-box control to work we don't need to add any source code. We can now run the program and it will display the selected image in the picture-box control.

For our last control let's look at a textbox control. A textbox control is similar to a label control except it is more powerful.

TEXTBOX CONTROL

A textbox control is like a label control in that the program can display text in it. The textbox control is more powerful in that the user can enter text in it while the program is running. Let's start by adding a textbox control and three label controls to our program.

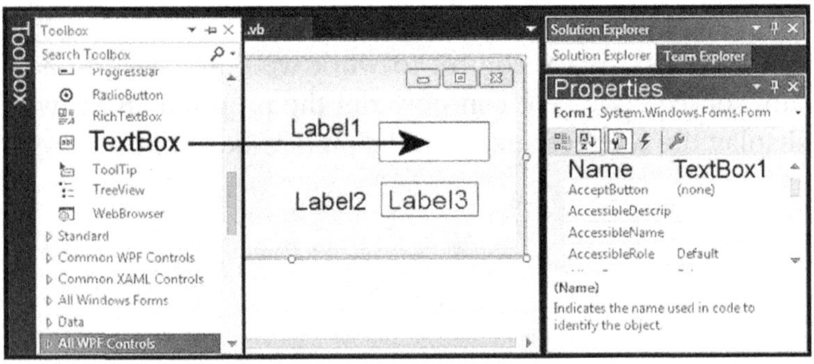

Let's set the following properties of the textbox control.

BorderStyle .. Change to (FixedSingle).

MaxLength .. This is the maximum number of characters the user can enter in the textbox. Let's set it to 10.

And for the three label controls, let's set the following properties.

Label1.BorderStyle = None
Label1.Text = Enter some text

Label2.BorderStyle .. None
Label2.Text = You entered

Label3.BorderStyle .. FixedSingle
Label3.Text = (blank)

Label3.MinimumSize .. Make the (MinimumSize) of Label3 the same as the (size) of the textbox control.

After setting the properties the form should look something like this.

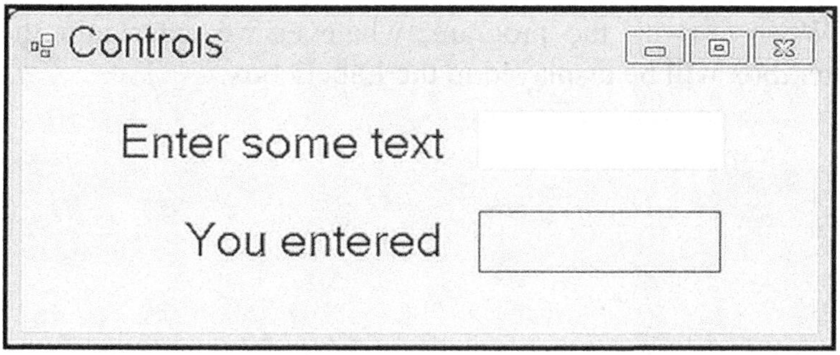

We want the program to take the text that the user enters into the textbox control and display it in the Label3 control.

TEXTBOX CONTROL SOURCE CODE

The place to put the source code is in the (Text-Changed) event of the (TextBox1) control. We want to set the text property of the Label3 control to whatever text is entered into the TextBox1 control. This can be done with the following line of code.

```
Label3.Text = TextBox1.Text
```

After we add this line of code to the TextBox1-TextChanged subroutine our program should look like this.

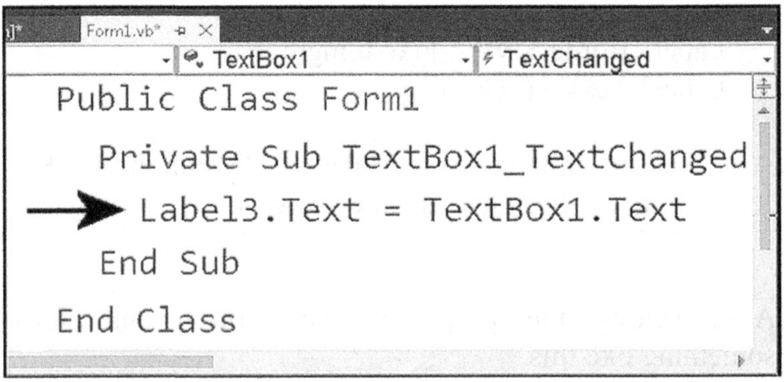

When we run the program, whatever we enter into the textbox will be displayed in the Label3 box.

The program works, but it does not do exactly what we want. Every time we type a letter the program displays that letter in the label box. It would be better if the program waits until we enter the full line of text and then press the Enter key before displaying the text. So, what we want is to put the line of code in the (Finished-Entering-Text) event of the (TextBox1) control. Well, sometimes we don't get what we want. Sadly, the creators of visual basic did not create a (Finished-Entering-Text) event. Since entering text is something we do a lot, programmers have come up with a workaround. We use another event of the textbox control called the Key-Down event.

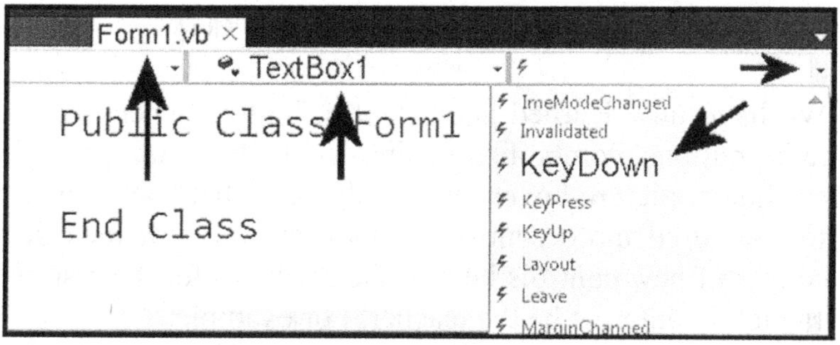

This event will be triggered each time the user presses a key. We need to add source code to this subroutine that will check to see if the user pressed the Enter key. If they did press the Enter key, then we want to display the textbox text in the label control. This line of code will do the trick.

```
If e.KeyCode = Keys.Enter  Then _
   Label3.Text = TextBox1.Text
```

After we add this line of code to the TextBox1-KeyDown event our program should look like this.

```
Form1.vb
TextBox1                                KeyDown
Public Class Form1
  Private Sub TextBox1_KeyDown(sender
    If e.KeyCode = Keys.Enter Then _
        Label3.Text = TextBox1.Text
  End Sub
End Class
```

This time, whatever we enter in the textbox won't be displayed in the label box until we press the Enter key.

SO MANY CONTROL - SO LITTLE TIME

We have now learned about labels, buttons, check-boxes, radio-buttons, combo-boxes, link-labels, list-views, month-calendars, picture-boxes, and textboxes. That leaves only a few hundred more controls to look at. We will look at a couple of new controls later in the book but for the rest, we can let the internet be the teacher. For example,

> If we do an internet search for "*visual basic how to use a progress bar control*", we can find websites and videos that show us how to use the progress-bar control.

MORE CONTROLS

So, what is next? A somewhat less flattering name for a software engineer is a computer programmer, and a somewhat less flattering name for a computer programmer is a coder. So let's learn some more code.

If at first you don't succeed ...
~~try try again~~
you must be a programmer.

Chapter 5
SOURCE CODE FOR CONTROLS

According to an expert, me, there are two types of source code statements, those dealing with a control and those that don't deal with a control. As I get older I wonder if I should keep calling myself an expert since (ex) is a has-been and (spert) is a drip under pressure? This chapter deals with source code statements that deal with controls.

In the previous chapters, we wrote two programs. The first program we wrote was the Hello program. The Hello program contained two controls, a label, and the form itself. The form control is the outer shell on which we place the other controls. The second program we wrote was the Controls program. On the Controls program, we had a button control, a calendar, a combo-box, a link-label, a list-view, a picture-box, and a textbox. For both programs, we followed a three-step process to add a control to the program.

1 .. In the form design frame, we dragged a control from the Toolbox frame to the form.

2 .. In the properties area of the form design frame, we specified the way we wanted the control to look, such as setting its background color to red.

3 .. In the code frame, we created a section of code called a subroutine that the program executed whenever the user did something to the control, such as clicking the control. We said that this section of code was set aside to handle the click event of the control.

SOURCE CODE FOR CONTROLS

In the previous chapters, we also learned that associated with each control there are properties and events. In this chapter, we will learn about a third feature of a control, methods.

Property .. an attribute of a control, such as its color
Event .. something the user can do to a control, such as clicking a button or entering text in a textbox.
Method .. something the program can do to a control, such as sort the items already in a combo-box.

Properties, such as the color of a button, can be set in the properties area of the form design frame. Properties can also be set or changed using source code in the program. In most cases, the source code to set or change a property can be located almost anywhere in the program. A control can have more than 20 properties but only a few properties are commonly used.

An event, such as clicking a button, causes the program to execute a specific section of code called a subroutine. A control can have more than 20 events but only a few events are commonly used.

A method, such as sorting the items in a combo-box, is a pre-written subroutine built into visual basic that the program can execute to do something to a control. In most cases, the source code to execute a method can be located almost anywhere in the program. A control can have more than 20 methods but only a few methods are commonly used.

PROPERTIES

The following is a list of properties that are common to several different types of controls, and how to set or check those properties using source code.

BackColor .. The following lines of code will set or check the background color of a control.

```
Button1.BackColor = Color.Red
IF Button1.BackColor = Color.Red  Then ...
```

Enabled .. The following line of code will disable a control. The control will still be visible, but it won't respond to anything the user does.

```
Button1.Enabled = False
IF Button1.Enabled = False  Then ...
```

Font .. The following lines of code will set the font type of whatever text is displayed in a control.

```
Label1.Font = New Font ("Lucida Handwriting",  10.0)
```

```
Label1.Font =
   New Font ("Arial Black",  10.0,  FontStyle.Bold)
```

ForeColor .. The following line of code will set the color of whatever text is displayed in a control.

```
Label1.ForeColor = Color.Red
```

Image, ImageAlign, TextImageRelation .. The following lines of code will display an image inside a control. Images of type (bmp), (icon), (gif), (wmf), and (jpeg) can be displayed in a control.

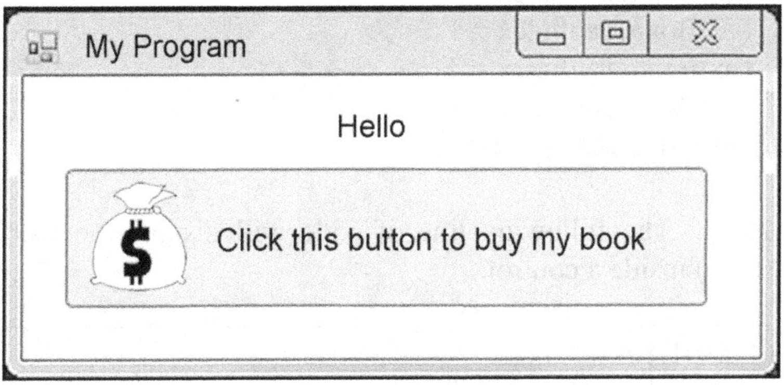

Button1.Image = Image.FromFile ("C:\FolderX\ImageY.bmp")
Button1.Text = "Click this button to buy my book"
Button1.ImageAlign = ContentAlignment.MiddleLeft
Button1.TextImageRelation = TextImageRelation.ImageBeforeText

TabIndex, TabStop .. As we add controls to our program visual basic automatically gives each control a tab index number, starting with index 0 of course. For simple programs, we can ignore the tab order. For a program designed to let the user fill in several textboxes with information, we may want to give the user the ability to use the (Tab) key to skip from one textbox to another. We may also want the program to tab to textboxes but not to other controls such as buttons.

We can use the following lines of code to let the user tab from TextBox2 to TextBox4 to TextBox1 to TextBox3 and then back to TextBox2.

```
TextBox2.TabIndex = 0
TextBox4.TabIndex = 1
TextBox1.TabIndex = 2
TextBox3.TabIndex = 3
Button1.TabStop = False
```

Text .. The following line of code will display the word (here) inside a control.

```
Label1.Text = "here"
IF Label1.Text = "here"   Then ...
```

Use-Mnemonic .. For me, hotkeys are what happens when I write lines of code really fast. For others, a hotkey, or shortcut key, is a way to click a button by using keyboard keys instead of having to use the mouse. In the following example, the user can click the (buy my book) button by just pressing the (Alt) key and the (B) key at the same time. The user knows it is the (B) key because the (b) in the word (buy) is underlined.

The following lines of code will make (Alt/B) a hotkey for the Button1 control.

```
Button1.Text = "Click this button to &buy my book"
Button1.UseMnemonic = True
```

To make a certain character in the Text property of a control a hotkey we just put an ampersand (&) in front of that character.

The first time I tested the program on my computer the (b) character was not underlined until I pressed (Alt/B). This seems to be a glitch in some versions of windows. I really wish Microsoft would consult with me before changing the way windows works. I used the following procedure to fix the glitch.

1 .. Open the Control Panel.
2 .. Select .. Ease of Access center.
3 .. Select .. Make the Keyboard easier to use.
4 .. Check .. Underline keyboard shortcuts.

Visible .. The following line of code will make a control disabled and invisible.

```
Button1.Visible = False
IF Button1.Visible = False   Then ...
```

EVENTS AND METHODS

The following is a list of events and methods that are common to several different types of controls.

Click events

The following events will let the user use the buttons on a mouse to get a control to do different things.

Click event .. The following event subroutine is triggered whenever the user clicks the Button1 control. By triggered we mean the program executes the source code in the subroutine.

```
Private Sub Button1_Click (sender As Object, e As Eve..
```

Double-Click event .. The following subroutine is triggered whenever the user double-clicks the Button1 control.

```
Private Sub Button1_DoubleClick (sender As Object, e ..
```

Right-Click event .. Since visual basic forgot to include a right-click event, responding to a mouse right-click has to be done in the button's (Mouse-Down) event.

```
Private Sub Button1_MouseDown (e As MouseEventArg
If e.Button = Windows.Forms.MouseButtons.Right Then
   code-to-execute
   End If
End Sub
```

Focus events

Sometimes, when we run a program, we see a flashing cursor on one of the controls. In programming jargon, we say that ControlX has the *focus*. Entering data into a textbox or using the tab key will switch the focus to a different control.

Got-Focus event .. The following subroutine is triggered whenever TextBox4 gets the focus.

```
Private Sub TextBox4_GotFocus (
```

Lost-Focus event .. The following subroutine is triggered whenever TextBox4 no longer has the focus.

```
Private Sub TextBox4_LostFocus (
```

Select method .. The following line of code will cause TextBox1 to have the focus.

```
TextBox1.Select ( )
```

The following lines of code will start the program with TextBox1 having the focus. These statements need to be in the (Form1-Load) event.

```
Private Sub Form1_Load (sender As Object, e As Event..
Me.Show ( )
TextBox1.Select ( )
```

Show method .. A program cannot set the focus until after the form is loaded. By default, the very last thing the (Form1-Load) event does is load the form. For this reason, we have to force the form to prematurely load using the (Me.Show) statement. If we are in Form1 then we have to refer to the Form1 control as (Me).

Active-Control property .. The following line of code will tell us which control currently has the focus.

```
IF Me.ActiveControl.Name = "TextBox1"   Then ...
```

Keyboard events

Suppose we want our program to know which keyboard key the user has pressed. Whether we use the (KeyPress) event or the (KeyUp) event depends on what the program is checking for. Regardless of the key we are checking for the following line of code needs to be in the (Form1-Load) event.

```
Private Sub Form1_Load (
KeyPreview = True
```

Key-Press event .. The following lines of code can be used to see if the user pressed the (a-z), (A-Z), or (0-9) key, or a special character key such as (.) or (?). These statements need to be in the (Form1-KeyPress) event.

```
Private Sub Form1_KeyPress (e As KeyPressEventArgs
If e.KeyChar = "a"  Then do something
If e.KeyChar = " "  Then do something
If e.KeyChar = "?"  Then do something
Label1.Text = e.KeyChar
```

Key-Up event .. The following lines of code can be used to see if the user pressed the (BackSpace), (Enter), (Escape), (F1), (Home), (Left-Arrow), or (Tab) key. When we enter the code (If e.KeyCode = Keys.) a drop-down list appears, and we can select the key we want to check for.

These statements need to be in the (Form1-KeyUp) event.

```
Private Sub Form1_KeyUp (e As KeyEventArgs)
If e.KeyCode = Keys.Tab   Then do something
If e.KeyCode = Keys.F1    Then do something
```

Key-Up event .. The following line of code can be used to see if the user pressed a hotkey, such as the (Alt) key and the (A) key at the same time. This statement needs to be in the (Form1-Key-Up) event.

```
Private Sub Form1_KeyUp (e As KeyEventArgs)
If (e.KeyCode = Keys.A)  And  (e.Alt = True)  Then ...
```

We already know that controls have a click event that is triggered when the user clicks on a control. What if we want to detect when the user moves the mouse over a control?

MouseMove events

Mouse-Hover event .. The following line of code will display a message in the Label1 box when the user holds the mouse over the Button1 control. This statement needs to be in the (Button1-Mouse-Hover) event.

```
Private Sub Button1_MouseHover (
Label1.Text = "Click this button, I dare you"
```

Mouse-Leave event .. Since we want the message to be displayed only when the mouse is over the Button1 control we need the following statement to erase the message when the mouse moves to some other control.

This statement needs to be in the (Button1-Mouse-Leave) event.

```
Private Sub Button1_MouseLeave (
Label1.Text = " "
```

PROPERTIES, EVENTS, AND METHODS

The previous examples are properties, events, and methods that are common to several different types of controls.

> The following is a list of properties, events, and methods that pertain to a specific type of control.

Button control

We already know that the button control has a click event, a subroutine that is triggered whenever the user clicks the button. We can also trigger the button's click event using source code in the program. The following line of code will trigger the Button1 click event whenever the TextBox1 control gets the focus. This statement needs to be in the (TextBox1-Got-Focus) event.

```
Private Sub TextBox1_GotFocus (sender As,  e As)
Call Button1_Click (nothing, nothing)
```

The reason there are two (nothing) words in the Call statement is because there are two variables in the subroutine statement, (sender) and (e).

Calendar control

In the previous chapter, we wrote a program called Controls. One of the controls we put in the Controls program was a month-calendar control. When the user selects a date from the month-calendar control the selected date is displayed in a label box.

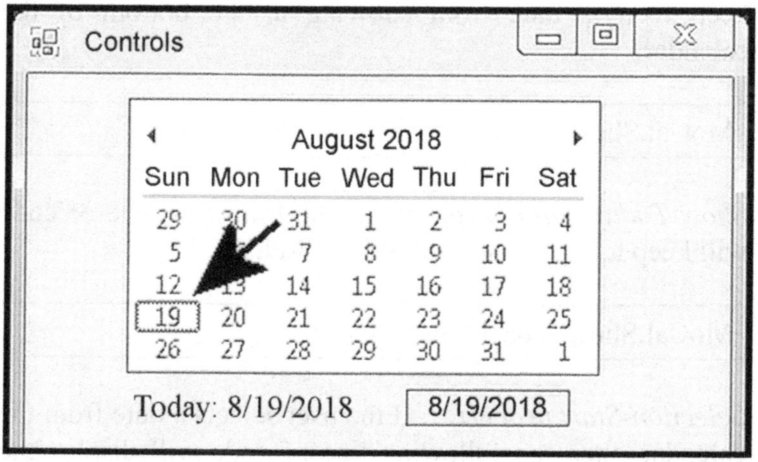

Here are some properties and events that pertain to a month-calendar control. Unless otherwise indicated, source code for a month-calendar control can go anywhere in the program. For simplicity, let's change the name of the MonthCalendar1 control to (MoCal).

Calendar-Dimensions property .. The following line of code will display the current year as a 2-column and 3-row calendar.

```
MoCal.SetCalendarDimensions = new Size (2, 4)
```

Min-Date property .. The following line of code will make today's date the first day shown on the calendar. The user will not be able to search backward from today's date.

```
MoCal.MinDate = Date.Today
```

Show-Today property .. The following line of code will keep today's date from showing at the bottom of the calendar.

```
MoCal.ShowToday = False
```

Show-Today-Circle property .. The following line of code will keep today's date from being circled.

```
MoCal.ShowTodayCircle = False
```

Selection-Start property .. If the user selects a date from the calendar, then the following line of code will display the selected date in the Label1 control. This statement needs to be in the (Date-Selected) event of the calendar control.

```
Private Sub MoCal_DateSelected (
Label1.Text = MoCal.SelectionStart
```

In the next chapter, we will see how to work with different date formats.

ComboBox control

In our Controls program, we also placed a combo-box control. A combo-box control allows the user to pull down a list of names and select one of the names.

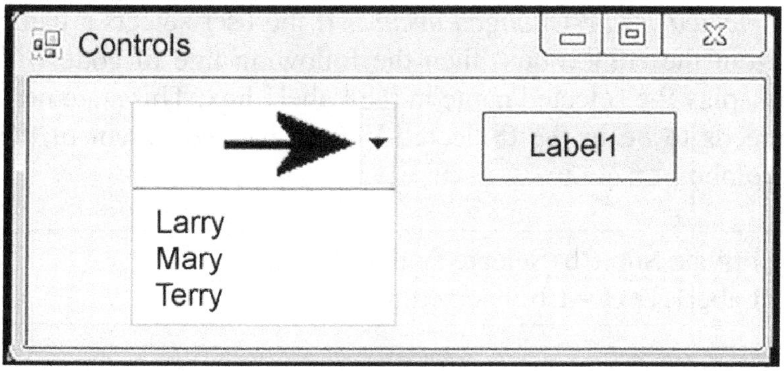

Here are some properties, events, and methods that pertain to a combo-box control. Unless otherwise indicated, source code for a combo-box control can go anywhere in the program. For simplicity, let's change the name of the ComboBox1 control to (Cb).

Items-Add method .. When we added the combo-box control we filled in the names using the (Items) property of the control. Here is how we can fill in the names using source code.

```
Cb.DropDownStyle = ComBoxStyle.DropDownList
Cb.Items.Add ("Peter")
Cb.Items.Add ("Paul")
Cb.Items.Add ("Mary")
```

Sorted property .. The following line of code will sort the names in the combo-box prior to displaying them.

```
Cb.Sorted = True
```

Selected-Value-Changed event .. If the user selects a name from the combo-box, then the following line of code will display the selected name in the Label1 box. This statement needs to be in the (Selected-Value-Changed) event of the combo-box control.

```
Private Sub Cb_SelectedValueChanged (
Label1.Text = Cb.SelectedItem
```

Items-Clear method .. The following line of code will delete the names in the combo-box.

```
Cb.Items.Clear ( )
```

ListView control

In our Controls program, we also added a list-view control. A list-view control allows the user to select a record from a table.

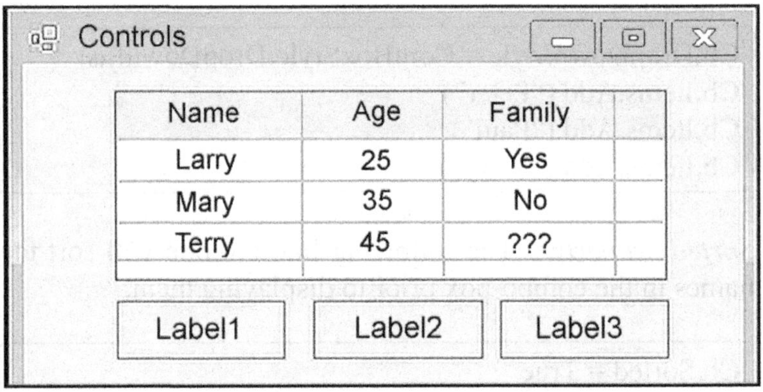

Here are some properties, events, and methods that pertain to a list-view control. Unless otherwise indicated, source code for a list-view control can go anywhere in the program. For simplicity, let's change the name of the ListView1 control to (Lv).

View property .. The following line of code is needed if we are going to store records in a list-view control.

```
Lv.View = View.Details
```

When we added the list-view control we filled in the records using the (Columns-Collection) property and the (Items-Collection) property of the control. Here is how we can fill in the records using source code.

Columns-Add method .. The following lines of code will create the three columns. The numbers determine the widths of the columns.

```
Lv.Columns.Add ("Name", 80)
Lv.Columns.Add ("Age", 60)
Lv.Columns.Add ("Family", 100)
```

Items-Add method .. The following lines of code will create the record for Larry.

```
Lv.Items.Add ("Larry")
Lv.Items(0).SubItems.Add (25)
Lv.Items(0).SubItems.Add ("Yes")
```

The following lines of code will create the record for Mary.

```
Lv.Items.Add ("Mary")
Lv.Items(0).SubItems.Add (35)
Lv.Items(0).SubItems.Add ("No")
```

And the following lines of code will create the record for Terry.

```
Lv.Items.Add ("Terry")
Lv.Items(0).SubItems.Add (45)
Lv.Items(0).SubItems.Add ("???")
```

Full-Row-Select property .. The following line of code will allow the user to select a table record by clicking anywhere in the record.

```
Lv.FullRowSelect = True
```

Grid-Lines property .. The following line of code will add grid lines to the table.

```
Lv.GridLines = True
```

Hide-Selection property .. The following line of code will keep the selected row highlighted even when the mouse is on another control.

```
Lv.HideSelection = False
```

Multi-Select property .. The following line of code will keep the user from selecting multiple rows at one time.

```
Lv.MultiSelect = False
```

Selected-Items property .. If the user selects a record from the table, then the following lines of code will display the selected record in three label boxes. The (Selected-Items.Count) statement tells us if the user has selected a record). These statements need to be in the (Selected-Index-Changed) event of the list-view control.

```
Private Sub Lv_SelectedIndexChanged (
If Lv.SelectedItems.Count > 0   Then
   Label1.Text = Lv.SelectedItems.Item(0).Text
   Label2.Text = Lv.SelectedItems(0).SubItems(1).Text
   Label3.Text = Lv.SelectedItems(0).SubItems(2).Text
   End If
```

Items-Remove-At method .. The following line of code will delete record 1, the second row, from the table. Remember that visual basic starts numbering at zero and not one.

```
Lv.Items.RemoveAt (1)
```

Items-Clear method .. The following line of code will delete all records from the table.

```
Lv.Items.Clear ( )
```

The next control is a new type of control that lets the user select a number from a range of numbers.

NumericUpDown control

The numeric-up-down control is added to the program just like any other control.

1 .. Make sure we are in the form design frame by clicking the tab (Form1.vb Design).

2 .. Click the word (Toolbox) and then the words (Common Controls).

3 .. Use the mouse to drag a (Numeric-Up-Down) control to the form design frame.

Using the numeric-up-down control the user can pick a number from a range of numbers by clicking the up or down arrows.

Here are some properties and events that pertain to a numeric-up-down control. Unless otherwise indicated, source code for a numeric-up-down control can go anywhere in the program. For simplicity, let's change the name of the NumericUpDown1 control to (NumUd).

Increment property .. The following line of code will increment the numbers by 10 as we click the up or down arrows.

```
NumUd.Increment = 10
```

Maximum property .. The following line of code sets 2050 as the biggest number in the range of numbers.

```
NumUd.Maximum = 2050
```

Minimum property .. The following line of code sets 1910 as the smallest number in the range of numbers.

```
NumUd.Minimum = 1910
```

Value property .. The following line of code sets 2018 as the starting number displayed in the control box.

```
NumUd.Value = 2018
```

Value property .. If the user uses the arrow keys to select a different number, the following line of code will display the selected number in the Label1 box. This statement needs to be in the (Value-Changed) event of the numeric-up-down control.

```
Private Sub NumUd_ValueChanged (
Label1.Text = NumUd.Value
```

Panel control

In a previous chapter, we learned that radio-buttons are mutually exclusive controls. When we check one radio-button visual basic uncheck the other radio-buttons. Suppose we want our program to have two radio-buttons to choose either male or female and two other radio-buttons to choose either resident or non-resident.

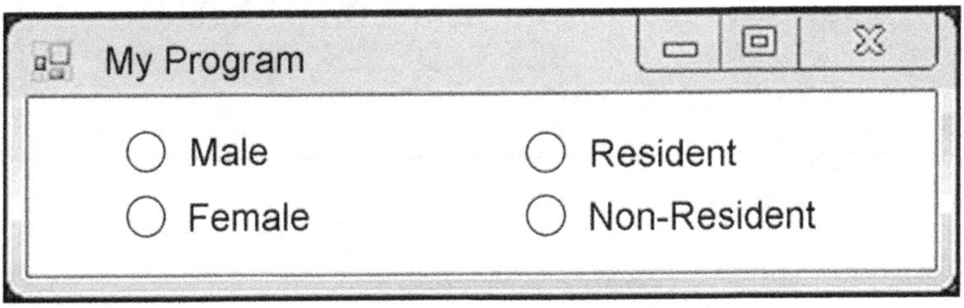

Four separate radio-buttons won't work. With four separate radio-buttons, we cannot specify a Female Resident. If we check Female visual basic will uncheck Resident and if we check Resident visual basic will uncheck Female. The solution is to use a new type of control called a panel control.

A Panel control is a container in which we can place other controls. Any controls we put inside a panel are independent of controls outside the panel. And if we have two panels then controls we put inside one panel are independent of controls we put inside the other panel.

Also, the controls inside a panel inherit the properties of the panel. If the set the visible property of the panel to False then the visible property of all the controls inside the panel is also False.

Therefore, the solution to our problem is to add two panels to our program and have the Male/Female radio-buttons in Panel1 and the Resident/Non-resident radio-buttons in Panel2.

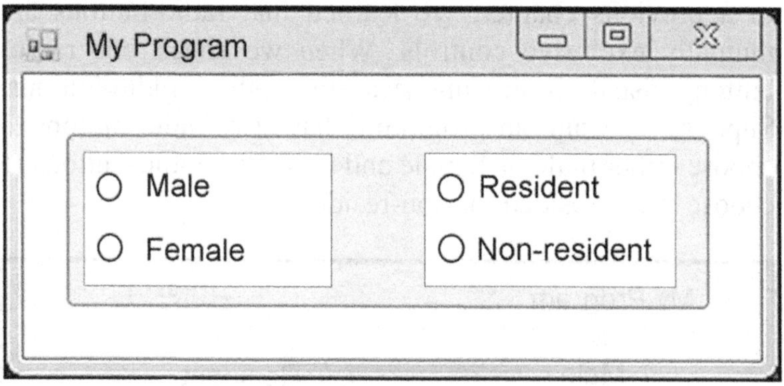

SOURCE CODE FOR CONTROLS

If we open the Common-Controls group of the Toolbox and find that there is no Panel control then we can do the following.

1 .. Open the Common-Controls group of the Toolbox.

2 .. Open the Containers group of the Toolbox.

3 .. Drag the Panel control from the Containers group to the Common-Controls group.

Here are some properties and events that pertain to a panel control. Unless otherwise indicated, source code for a panel control can go anywhere in the program. For simplicity, let's call the four radio-buttons RbMale, RbFemale, RbRes, and RbNonRes..

Border-Style property .. The following line of code will add a border to a panel control.

```
Panel1.BorderStyle = BorderStyle.FixedSingle
```

Checked property .. The following line of code will start the program with the Male radio-button already checked.

```
RbMale.Checked = True
```

Checked property .. We can use the following lines of code to display the Male/Female selection in Label1 and the Resident/Non-resident selection in Label2.

This statement needs to be in the (Checked-Changed) event of the Radio-Button-Male control.

```
Private Sub RbMale_CheckedChanged (
If RbMale.Checked  Then Label1.Text = "Male"
```

This statement needs to be in the (Checked-Changed) event of the Radio-Button-Female control.

```
Private Sub RbFemale_CheckedChanged (
If RbFemale.Checked  Then Label1.Text = "Female"
```

This statement needs to be in the (Checked-Changed) event of the Radio-Button-Resident control.

```
Private Sub RbRes_CheckedChanged (
If RbRes.Checked  Then Label2.Text = "Resident"
```

And this statement needs to be in the (Checked-Changed) event of the Radio-Button-NonResident control.

```
Private Sub RbNonRes_CheckedChanged (
If RbNonRes.Checked  Then Label2.Text = "Non-Res"
```

What if we have 100 different radio-buttons? Do we need to put source code in 100 different Checked-Changed event subroutines? Fortunately, there is a shortcut. When we created the Checked-Changed event subroutine for the Radio-Button-Male control visual basic wrote the first line of code for us.

```
Private Sub RbMale_CheckedChanged (
  sender As Object,   e As EventArgs) _
  Handles RbMale.CheckedChanged
```

The last part of the statement says that this subroutine handles the Check-Changed event of the RbMale control. All we need to do is indicate that this subroutine also handles the Check-Changed event of the other radio-button controls.

```
Private Sub RbMale_CheckedChanged (
   sender As Object,   e As EventArgs) _
   Handles RbMale.CheckedChanged,
   RbFemale.CheckedChanged,
   RbRes.CheckedChanged,
   RbNonRes.CheckedChanged
```

Now, we can check which of the four radio-buttons have been checked in this one subroutine. Our program should now look like this.

```
Private Sub RbMale_CheckedChanged (
   sender As Object,   e As EventArgs) _
   Handles RbMale.CheckedChanged,
   RbFemale.CheckedChanged,
   RbRes.CheckedChanged,
   RbNonRes.CheckedChanged
   '---------------------------------------------
   If RbMale.Checked Then Label1.Text = "Male"
   If RbFemale.Checked Then Label1.Text = "Female"
   If RbRes.Checked Then Label2.Text = "Resident"
   If RbNonRes.Checked Then Label2.Text = "Non-resident"
End Sub
```

When we run the program and check the Female and Resident radio-buttons our choices will show up in the two label boxes.

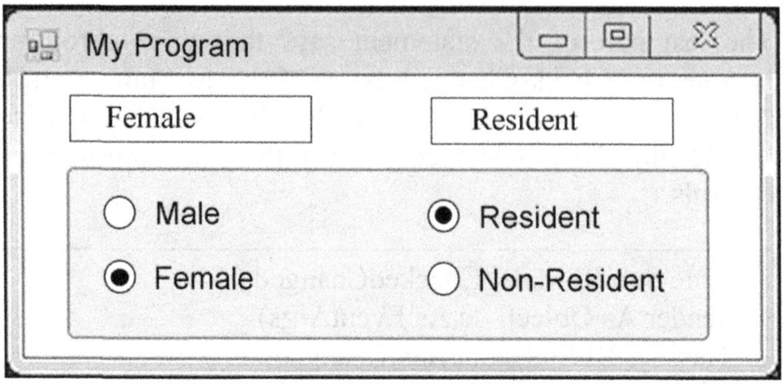

In a previous chapter, we learned how to use the Link-Label control to access a website on the internet. We can use a picture-box control to display an image from the internet inside our program.

PictureBox control

Here are some properties that pertain to a picture-box control. Unless otherwise indicated, source code for a picture-box control can go anywhere in the program. For simplicity, let's change the name of the PictureBox1 control to (PicBox).

Prior to loading an internet image into a picture-box control, we need to locate the image on the internet and save its (http://) internet address.

Image-Location property .. The following line of code will display an internet image inside a picture-box control.

```
PicBox.ImageLocation =
  "http://www.WebSiteX.com/ImageY.jpg"
```

Size-Mode property .. The following line of code will make sure the image fits inside the picture-box control.

```
PicBox.SizeMode = PictureBoxSizeMode.StretchImage
```

When we run the program, we will see the image displayed in the picture-box control.

Suppose we want our program to count to infinity. In my math book, "*Calm Down! Its Only Math*", I show that there is actually more than one infinity. Even with a fast computer counting to infinity may take some time so we probably need to let the user know how the counting process is going. Our next new control will do that.

Progress-Bar control

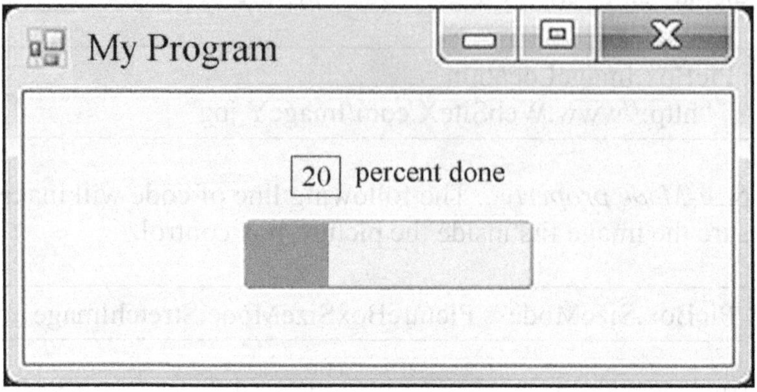

The progress-bar control will track the status of the counting-to-infinity process. We can configure the control so that every time 10 percent of the counting process is completed the progress-bar will increment one step. This will show the status of the counting process from 0 percent done to 100 percent done.

Here are some properties and methods that pertain to a progress-bar control. Unless otherwise indicated, source code for a progress-bar control can go anywhere in the program. For simplicity, let's change the name of the ProgressBar1 control to (ProgBar).

Maximum property .. The following line of code sets 100 percent as the upper limit of the progress-bar.

```
ProgBar.Maximum = 100
```

Minimum property .. The following line of code sets 0 percent as the lower limit of the progress-bar.

```
ProgBar.Minimum = 0
```

Step property .. The following line of code will increment the progress-bar in 10 equal steps. Each step will therefore represent 10 percent of the process being completed.

```
ProgBar.Step = 10
```

Value property .. The following line of code will display the current value of the progress-bar in a label box.

```
Label1.Text = ProgBar.Value
```

Perform-Step method .. We have to use our own code to determine how much of the counting process is done and when it is time to increment the progress-bar. Every time an additional 10 percent of the counting process is completed the following line of code will increment the progress-bar one step.

```
ProgBar.PerformStep ( )
```

Suppose we want our program to inform the user about the complicated topic of infinity, answering such questions as, if we count to infinity once, then do we ever need to do it again? The textbox control can display a small amount of information, but we need a control that is more powerful.

Rich Textbox control

The rich-textbox control is like a mini word processor. We can have an area inside our program that is as powerful as the Windows Notepad program.

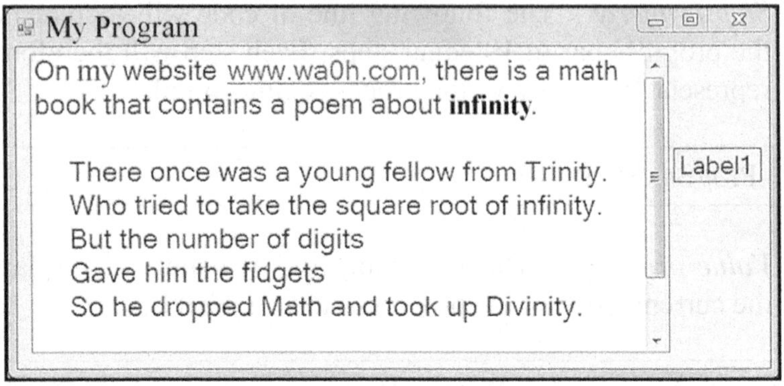

Here are some properties and methods that pertain to a rich-textbox control. Unless otherwise indicated, source code for a rich-textbox control can go anywhere in the program. For simplicity, let's change the name of the RichTextBox1 control to (RichTb).

Clear method .. The following line of code will erase whatever is in a rich-textbox control.

```
RichTb.Clear ( )
```

The following line of code will display a paragraph in a rich-textbox control.

```
RichTb.SelectedText = "Paragraph 1 Abc"
```

The following lines of code will highlight the number 1 in the paragraph above.

```
RichTb.SelectedText = "Paragraph 1 Abc"
RichTb.SelectionStart = 10
RichTb.SelectionLength = 1
RichTb.SelectionColor = Color.Red
```

In place of the (Color.Red) statement, we can have any of the following statements.

```
RichTb.SelectedText = "Paragraph 1 Abc"
RichTb.SelectionStart = 10
RichTb.SelectionLength = 1
RichTb.SelectionFont =
   New Font(RichTextBox1.Font,  FontStyle.Bold)
RichTb.SelectionFont =
   New Font(RichTextBox1.Font,  FontStyle.Underline)
RichTb.SelectionFont =
   New Font(RichTextBox1.Font,  FontStyle.Italic)
```

When text is displayed in a rich-textbox the text automatically wraps from one line to the next. The following lines of code show how to use code to skip to the next line.

```
RichTb.SelectedText = "Line 1"
RichTb.AppendText (Chr(13) & Chr(10))
RichTb.SelectedText = "Line 2"
```

The following lines of code show how to indent a paragraph.

```
RichTb.SelectedText = “Paragraph 1 Abc”
RichTb.AppendText (Chr(13) & Chr(10))
RichTb.SelectedText = “Paragraph 2 is indented”
RichTb.SelectionIndent = 20
```

The following lines of code show how to center-align a paragraph.

```
RichTb.SelectedText = “Paragraph 1 Abc”
RichTb.AppendText (Chr(13) & Chr(10))
RichTb.SelectedText = “Paragraph 2 is centered”
RichTb.SelectionAlignment =
   HorizontalAlignment.Center
```

Detect-Urls property .. The following line of code will convert internet link text, such as (www.wa0h.com), to an internet link.

```
RichTb.DetectUrls = True
```

Process-Start method .. If the user clicks an internet link that is contained in a rich-textbox control, then the following line of code will bring up the website. This statement needs to be in the (Link-Clicked) event of the rich-textbox control.

```
Private Sub RichTb_LinkClicked (
Process.Start (e.LinkText)
```

Read-Only property .. The following line of code will make the text in a rich-textbox read-only, meaning the user cannot alter the text.

```
RichTb.ReadOnly = True
```

We are already familiar with how a simple textbox control works but there are a couple of features worth mentioning.

TextBox control

Here are a couple of properties that pertain to a textbox control. Unless otherwise indicated, source code for a textbox control can go anywhere in the program.

Character-Casing property .. The following line of code will cause anything typed into a textbox be automatically converted to upper case letters.

```
TextBox1.CharacterCasing = CharacterCasing.Upper
```

Password-Char property .. The following line of code will cause anything typed into a textbox be automatically converted to an (*). This is how enter-your-password fields are created.

```
TextBox1.PasswordChar = "*"
```

The last two controls we need to look at are a little different in that they don't appear in the program. The first is a control that lets the program hold off executing some code until an interval of time has passed.

Timer control

A timer control, which is invisible to the user, lets the program automatically execute some code every time a certain interval of time has passed. This will allow our program to execute a section of code every second or every minute or every hour.

If we open the Common-Controls group of the Toolbox and find that there is no Timer control, then we can do the following.

1 .. Open the Common-Controls group of the Toolbox.

2 .. Open the All-Windows-Forms group of the Toolbox.

3 .. Drag the Timer control from the All-Windows-Forms group to the Common-Controls group.

When we drag a timer control from the Toolbox to the form design frame it shows up at the bottom of the frame.

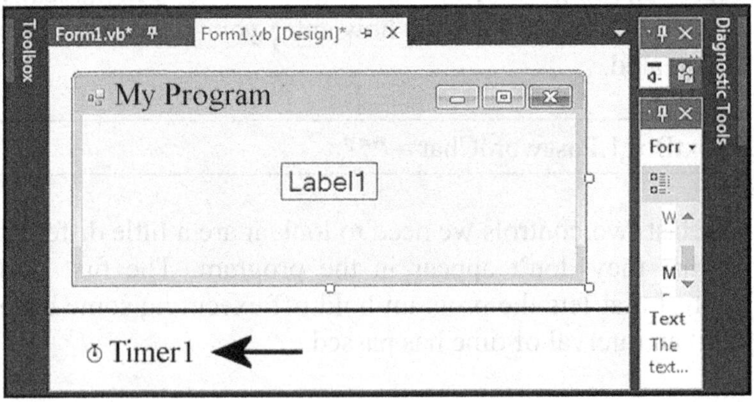

Here are some properties, events, and methods that pertain to a timer control. Unless otherwise indicated, source code for a timer control can go anywhere in the program.

Interval property .. The following line of code will cause the timer control to trigger the (Timer1-Tick) section of code every 1000 milliseconds, which is every second.

```
Timer1.Interval = 1000
```

Start method .. The following line of code will turn the timer control on. We can also start the timer by setting its enabled property to True.

```
Timer1.Start ( )
```

Tick event .. The following line of code will display the current time in a label box every second. This statement needs to be in the (Tick) event of the timer control.

```
Private Sub Timer1_Tick (
Label1.Text = TimeOfDay
```

Another invisible control that shows up at the bottom of the form design frame is the ToolTip control.

ToolTip control

Earlier we saw how to use the mouse-hover event to display a message in one control whenever the user holds the mouse over another control. Suppose we want to display a message in a pop-up message box whenever the user holds the mouse over a control. We can display pop up messages by using the tooltip control.

If the tooltip control is not in the Common-Controls group of the Toolbox, we can drag it there from the All-Windows-Forms group of the Toolbox, just like we did with the timer control. When we drag the tooltip control from the Toolbox to the form design frame, it will, like the timer control, show up at the bottom of the frame.

Here are some properties and methods that pertain to a tooltip control. Unless otherwise indicated, source code for a tooltip control can go anywhere in the program.

Initial-Delay property .. The following line of code will display the tooltip message after 100 milliseconds or 1/10th of a second.

```
ToolTip1.InitialDelay = 100
```

Set-ToolTip method .. The following line of code will display the specified tooltip message whenever the mouse is held over the Label1 control.

```
ToolTip1.SetToolTip (Label1, “This is label box 1”)
```

In this chapter, we have learned about a few of the many control properties, methods, and events. The internet is a wonderful source of information on what the other properties, methods, and events do.

Only two more chapters to go, and believe it or not, we know very little about writing source code. So far, our programs have a lot of bells and whistles, but they don’t do anything. It is time to learn visual basic and write some code.

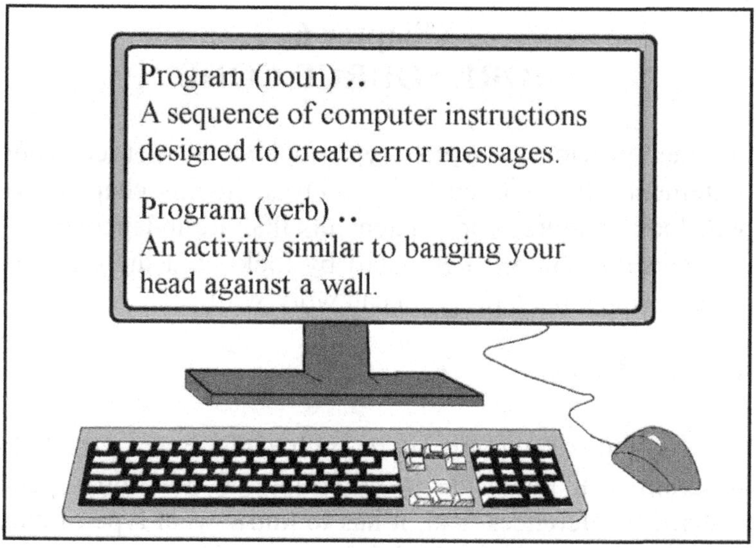
Program (noun) ..
A sequence of computer instructions designed to create error messages.
Program (verb) ..
An activity similar to banging your head against a wall.

Chapter 6
MORE SOURCE CODE

In the previous chapter, we looked at source code statements that worked with controls. In this chapter, we will look at source code statements that are independent of any specific control. Let's start by looking at the different types of data that a program can work with.

DATA TYPES

All computer programs work with data. Even our Hello program contained the word Hello. If a source code statement references data, it has to know what type of data it is referencing, a group of characters, a number, or a date. Following are some of the different types of data that a program can work with.

Strings

A string is nothing more than a group of characters. We tell a program that a group of characters is a string by putting the characters inside quotes. The following are examples of strings.

1	“ ”
2	“AaBbCc .. 1,2,3 .. # $?”

In visual basic, the number of characters we can have in a string is virtually unlimited. Strings and numbers are probably the two most common types of data found in a program.

Numbers

There are two basic types of numbers in visual basic, numbers that contain a decimal point and numbers that don't contain a decimal point.

integer .. A number without a decimal point.

largest	2,147,483,647 (2 billion)
smallest	-2,147,483,648 (-2 billion)

long .. A really big number without a decimal point.

largest	9,223,372,036,854,775,807
smallest	-9,223,372,036,854,775,808

single .. A number that contains a decimal point.

largest positive	34028235+(31 zeros).0
smallest positive	0.(44 zeros)1401298
largest negative	-34028235+(31 zeros).0
smallest negative	-0.(44 zeros)1401298

double .. A gigantic number with a decimal point.

largest +	17976931348623157+(292 zeros).0
smallest +	0.(323 zeros)494065645841246544
largest -	-17976931348623157+(292 zeros).0
smallest -	-0.(323 zeros)494065645841246544

real .. A real number is another term for a number that contains a decimal point. Single numbers and double numbers are both real numbers.

Boolean .. (True, False)

A Boolean data element has two possible values, True or False. If we define (Weekend) as a Boolean data element, then the following two (IF) statement produce the same results.

If Weekend = True Then do this
If Weekend Then do this

DateTime .. 12/31/2018 11:59:59 PM

A date-time data element is composed of (year/month/day) components and (hour/minute/second) components.

largest	12/31/9999 11:59:59 (look out for Y10K)
smallest	01/01/0001 00:00:00

Later on in this chapter we will learn how to work with these different types of data. With our Hello program we had one piece of data, the string "Hello". With our Controls program, we had a list-view control that contained both string data and integer data. As our programs become more complex it will be easier to work with data if we give the data easy to remember names. To name data elements we use *variables*.

VARIABLES

The list-view control in the Controls program had three records, Larry, Mary, and Terry. Each record contained three pieces of data, Name, Age, and Family-status.

Name	Age	Family-status
Larry	25	Yes
Mary	35	No
Terry	45	???

In the Controls program, we referred to a person's name as *ListView1.SelectedItems.Item (0)*. If we refer to a person's name several times in a program, it will be easier if we create a variable called (TheirName). Think of a variable as a box in which we can put different, but related, data. Sometimes the variable TheirName will contain the string Larry, sometimes it will contain the string Mary, and sometimes it will contain the string Terry. Once we put a person's name in the variable TheirName we can thereafter refer to the person's name as TheirName. We can also create a variable called (TheirAge) to hold the age of a person and a third variable called (TheirFamilyStatus) to hold the family-status of a person.

To create a variable, we use a *dimension* (Dim) statement. When we use a Dim statement to create a variable we have to tell visual basic what type of data we plan to store in the variable. The following table shows how to create a variable and store a value in the variable.

1	Dim a As String	a = "Good morning"
2	Dim i As Integer	i = -123
3	Dim LongVar As Long	LongVar = 12345678
4	Dim Sing As Single	Sing = -1.23
5	Dim Dv As Double	Dv = 12345.67890
6	Dim Tf As Boolean	Tf = True
7	Dim DateX As Date	DateX = "Jan 2, 2018"
8	Dim a, b, c As String	
9	Dim Name As String = "Hi"	

Lines 1-7 create variables for different data types.

Line 7 is a Date variable. A date variable can hold a date, a time, or a date and time.

Line 8 creates three string variables at once.

Line 9 creates a string variable and stores "Hi" in it.

The following rules apply to the name we give a variable.

The name must begin with (a-z) or (A-Z).

The name must contain only (a-z), (A-Z) or (1-9).
No spaces allowed.

The name must be less than 1024 characters.

Now that we know what strings are and how to create them let's see some of the stuff we can do with a string.

STRINGS

The following lines of code will store a value in a string.

statement	results
StringX = “abc” StringX = “3.14159”	“abc” “3.14159”

& .. The following line of code will join 3 strings into one long string.

StringX = “Hi” & “ ” & “there”	“Hi there”

To-String .. The following lines of code will convert numbers, or other types of data, into a string.

StringX = IntegerX.ToString	“-123”
StringX = SingleX.ToString	“3.14159”
StringX = BooleanTf.ToString	“False”
StringX = DateTimeX.ToString	“10/8/2018 1:56:28”

The following lines of code show different ways we can use (To-String) to format a number. For other ways to format a number, search the internet for “*visual basic 2017 formatting a string*”.

Dim x As Single = 3.14159 Label1.Text = x.ToString (“##,###.##”)	“3.14”
Dim x As Integer = -123 Label1.Text = x.ToString (“##,###.00”)	“-123.00”

Pad-Left .. The following lines of code will put spaces, or some other character, in front of a string until the string is 7 characters long.

StringX = "abc" StringY = StringX.PadLeft (7)	" abc"
IntegerX = -123 StringY = IntegerX.ToString.PadLeft (7)	" -123"
StringX = "abc" StringY = StringX.PadLeft (7, "-")	"----abc"

The middle example shows how (To-String) and (Pad-Left) can be combined in the same statement. There is also a (*Pad-Right*) statement.

To-Lower .. The following lines of code will convert a string to all upper-case letters or all lower-case letters.

StringX = "aBc" StringY = StringX.ToUpper StringY = StringX.ToLower	 "ABC" "abc"

Trim .. The following lines of code will remove any spaces that are at the beginning or the end of a string.

StringX = " aBc " StringY = StringX.TrimStart StringY = StringX.TrimEnd StringY = StringX.Trim	 "aBc " " abc" "aBc"

Length .. The following line of code will get the length of a string.

StringX = " aBc " IntegerX = StringX.Length	8

Starts-With .. The following lines of code will check to see what a string starts with or ends with.

StringX = "aBc" If StringX.StartsWith ("aB") Then ... If StringX.StartsWith ("ab") Then ...	it does it does not

If StringX.StartsWith ("ab",
  StringComparison.
  CurrentCultureIgnoreCase)   Then ...
	it does

Most statements that involve strings are *case-sensitive*, meaning visual basic considers an upper-case (B) to be different than a lower-case (b). The second example tells visual basic to consider upper-case characters and lower-case characters as being the same characters. There is also a corresponding (*Ends-With*) statement.

Index-Of .. The following lines of code will find the position of a group of characters that are part of a string. The position of the first character is position zero.

1 2 3	StringX = "aBc zBc" IntegerX = StringX.IndexOf ("bc") IntegerX = StringX.IndexOf ("Bc")	 -1 1
4	IntegerX = StringX.LastIndexOf ("Bc")	5

Line 2 finds the position of the first occurrence of (bc). (-1) means that (bc) is not part of StringX. Remember that most statements that involve strings are *case-sensitive.*

Line 4 finds the position of the last occurrence of characters (Bc).

Sub-String .. The following lines of code will extract characters from a string.

StringX = "aBc DeF"	
'extract characters starting at position 2 StringY = StringX.Substring (2)	"c DeF"
'extract 2 character starting at position 0 StringY = StringX.Substring (0, 2)	"aB"

Replace .. The following lines of code will replace certain characters in a string with other characters.

StrX = "aBc ABC"	
'replace all (B)s with (b)s StrY = StrX.Replace ("B", "b")	"abc AbC"
'replace all (ABC)s with (aBc)s StrY = StrX.Replace ("ABC", "aBc")	"aBc aBc"

Insert .. The following line of code will insert 2 dashes into a string, starting at position 3.

StringX = "aBc ABC" StringY = StringX.Insert (3, "--")	"abc-- AbC"

Remove .. The following lines of code will remove certain characters from a string.

StringX = "aBc AbC" 'remove all characters starting at position 3 StringY = StringX.Remove (3)	"aBc"
'remove 4 chars starting at position 2 StringY = StringX.Remove (2, 4)	"aBC"

If we do an internet search for "*visual basic 2017 strings*", we can find websites and videos that show other stuff that can be done with strings.

Programmers are nerds and nerds love to do math, so let's see some of the stuff we can do with numbers and math.

NUMBERS AND MATH

Yes, it is true, math stands for (M)ental (A)buse (T)o (H)umans. The following lines of code show the types of math operations we can do in visual basic. Assume that (X), (Y), and (Z) are numbers.

Z = X + Y	addition
Z = X - Y	subtraction
Z = X * Y	multiplication
Z = X / Y	division
Z = X ^ Y	(X) to the power of (Y)

The following lines of code show how to convert numbers from one data type to another data type.

‘convert an integer to a single type SingleX = Convert.ToSingle (IntegerX)	
‘convert an integer to a double type DoubleX = Convert.ToDouble (IntegerX)	
‘convert a single to an integer type IntegerX = Cint (123.789)	124
‘convert a single to an integer type IntegerX = Math.Truncate (123.789)	123

( ), [ ], an { } can be used to group operations together.

```
Z = {A + [ (B-C) / (D-E) ] * (F^G) }  + 1.234
```

Mod .. The following line of code shows how to do modular arithmetic.

Z = 5 mod 3	2 (the remainder of 5/3)

The following are math constants built into visual basic.

Z = Math.E	2.71828182
Z = Math.Pi	3.14159265

Math functions .. If we type (Z = Math.), a list drops down and we can choose from several different math functions.

Z = Math.Abs (X) Z = Math.Log (X)	absolute value of X natural logarithm of X

Random numbers .. The following lines of code will create a random number between 1 and 6.

```
Randomize ( )
IntegerX = Cint (Math.Truncate ( (6 * Rnd ( ) ) + 1) )
```

Earlier we mentioned the (Date) data type. Here are some of the things we can do with a date or time.

DATE-TIME

Now, Today, TimeOfDay .. The following lines of code will display the current date or time.

Label2.Text = Today Label2.Text = TimeOfDay Label2.Text = Now	1/2/2018 1:02:03 PM 1/2/2018 1:02:03 PM

The following lines of code can be used to store a date or time in a date type variable.

Dim DateX As Date DateX = "01/02/18" DateX = "Jan 2, 2018" DateX = "January 2, 2018"	 1/2/2018 1/2/2018 1/2/2018
DateX = "1:02" DateX = "1:02 pm" DateX = "13:02"	1:02:00 AM 1:02:00 PM 1:02:00 PM
DateX = "1/2/18 1:02 PM"	1/2/2018 1:02:00 PM

Format .. The following lines of code can be used to display a date or time in different formats.

```
Dim DateX As Date = "Jan 2, 2018"
Label2.Text = Format (DateX,  "yyyy-MM-dd")
'displays .. 2018-01-02
```

```
Label2.Text = Format (Today,  "d/M/yy")
'displays .. 2/1/18
```

```
Label2.Text = Format (Now, "dddd, MMMM dd, yyyy")
'displays .. Monday, January 02, 2018
```

```
Dim DateX As Date = "1:02 PM"
Label2.Text = Format (DateX,  "HH:mm")
'displays .. 01:02
```

```
Label2.Text = Format (TimeOfDay,  "hh:mm")
'displays .. 01:02
```

```
Label2.Text = Format (Now,  "HH:mm:ss tt")
'displays .. 13:02:00 PM
```

```
Dim DateX As Date = "1/2/18  3:04 AM"
Label2.Text = Format (DateX, "M/d/yyyy  H:mm:tt")
'displays .. 1/2/2018  3:04 AM
```

When formatting the date, the following codes can be used.

code	displays
M, MM, MMM, MMMM d, dd, ddd, dddd yy, yyyy	(month) 1, 01, Jan, January (day) 2, 02, Mon, Monday (year) 18, 2018

When formatting the time, the following codes can be used.

code	displays
h, hh	(hour) 3, 03 (12-hour clock)
H, HH	(hour) 3, 03 (24-hour clock)
m, mm	(minute) 4, 04
ss	(second) 05
tt	AM, PM

If we do an internet search for "*visual basic 2017 date time format codes*", we can find websites that show other ways to format a date or time.

The following lines of code can be used to extract different parts of a date or time.

Dim DateX As Date = "1/2/18 3:04 AM"	
i = DatePart (DateInterval.Month, DateX)	1
i = DatePart (DateInterval.Day, DateX)	2
i = DatePart (DateInterval.Year, DateX)	2018
i = DatePart (DateInterval.Hour, DateX)	3

Besides month, day, and year, we can also extract the (Hour), (Minute), and (Second). We can also extract the (DayOfYear).

Is-Date .. The following line of code will determine if a string contains a valid date.

```
If IsDate (StringX)   Then ...
```

AddDays .. The following lines of code can be used to determine a future date.

Dim DateX As Date = “2/28/2016” Label2.Text = DateX.AddDays (1) Label2.Text = DateX.AddYears (65)	 2/29/2016 2/28/2081

In the previous chapter, we learned how to insert an image from the internet into a Picture-Box control. Suppose we want to insert an image which is stored on our computer into a Picture-Box control.

IMAGES

The following lines of code will insert an image which is stored on our computer into a Picture-Box control.

```
Dim PicX As New Bitmap (“C:\DirX\MyPic.jpg”)
PicBox1.SizeMode = PictureBoxSizeMode.StretchImage
PicBox1.Image = PicX
```

We know how to use a variable to store data such as a person’s name. The problem is, a variable can hold only one name at a time. What if we want to have access to thousands of names at the same time.

ARRAYS

An array is a bunch of variables, all with the same name, used to store related data items, such as a person’s name.

TheirName (0)	TheirName (1)	TheirName (2)
Peter	Paul	Mary

If the name of the array is (TheirName), then by default the 1st person's name is stored in TheirName (0) because visual basic like to start counting things at zero and not one. The 3rd person's name is stored in TheirName (2). The following lines of code show how to create an array using a dimension statement.

```
1  Dim TheirName (3) As String
2  Dim ArrayX ( ) As Single = { 0,  1,  -2.3,  3.14 }
```

Line 1 creates an array that holds 4 items, item 0 through item 3. Creating an array that holds 4 items allows us to override the default and store the 1st person's name in TheirName (1) and the 3rd person's name in TheirName (3).

Line 2 is a way to create an array and fill it with data at the same time. Visual basic will automatically determine the dimension size of the array.

The following lines of code will store the names of the three people in array TheirName.

```
TheirName (1) = “Peter”
TheirName (2) = “Paul”
TheirName (3) = “Mary”
```

ReDim-Preserve .. The following line of code will make the TheirName array bigger, even after it has been created and filled with data.

```
ReDim Preserve TheirName (10)
```

Length .. The following line of code will tell us the size of the TheirName array.

```
Label2.Text = TheirName.Length
```

Array.Sort .. The following line of code will sort the items stored in the TheirName array.

```
Array.Sort (TheirName)
```

Array.Reverse .. The following line of code will reverse the items stored in the TheirName array.

```
Array.Reverse (TheirName)
```

Array.IndexOf .. The following lines of code will tell us which positions of the TheirName array contain the first and last occurrence of the item (Paul).

i = Array.IndexOf (TheirName, “paul”)	-1
i = Array.IndexOf (TheirName, “Paul”)	2
i = Array.LastIndexOf (TheirName, “Paul”)	2

The (-1) in the first example means that the array does not contain the item (paul). Strings are case sensitive and (paul) is not the same as (Paul).

Array.Clear .. The following line of code will delete the 4 items stored in the TheirName array.

```
Array.Clear (TheirName, 0, 4)
```

MORE SOURCE CODE

Before we get any deeper into programming this might be a good time to learn what to do when we test our program and the program does not work the way we want it to.

DEBUGGING

We learned in a previous chapter that sometimes when we run our program an (Error-List) opens at the bottom of the coding frame telling us that there is a bug in the program.

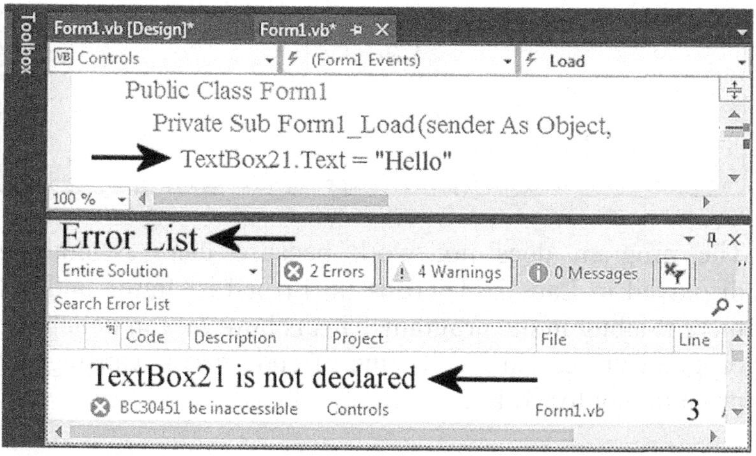

This program will not work because we forgot to create a TextBox21 control. Some errors are harder to find. Consider the following program.

```
Dim i As Integer
Dim s As String = “John Doe”
Dim ss As String
i = s.Length
ss = s.SubString (6, 3)
Label2.Text = ss
```

The purpose of this program is to display in Label2 the last 3 characters of the string (John Doe). The length of string (s) is 8 characters, so we want to display characters 6, 7, and 8. When we run this program we get the following results.

The program does not work because there is nothing displayed in Label2. There is no Error-List frame and yet there is a bug in the program. This is how we can debug the program or zero in on the line of code that is causing the program not to work.

1 .. Have the program stop when it gets to line 4.
i = s.Length

2 .. Have the program execute one line at a time.

3 .. At each step, see what is stored in each variable.

By having the program execute one line at a time we can find the line that is causing the problem.

To have the program stop running when it gets to line 4 we set a *breakpoint* at line 4. To set a breakpoint at line 4 we do the following.

1 .. Put the cursor at the start of line 4

2 .. Click the word (Debug) in the menu bar and then click (Toggle Breakpoint), or just press (F9). When a breakpoint is set, the line of code turns red.

Now, let's test the program. The program will stop on line 4. Don't be alarmed if there is no program output.

Have the program do line 4 by pressing the F8 key.

To see the results of executing line 4, hold the mouse over the (i) in line 4. Visual basic will show us that the length (i) of string (s) is (8). Line 4 is working OK.

To see what is stored in the other variables just click the word (Debug) in the menu bar and then click (Windows) and then click (Locals).

Have the program execute line 5 by pressing F8.

At this point, the program finishes but Label2 does not contain (Doe). This tells us the problem is probably line 5, [*ss = s.SubString (6, 3)*].

Line 5 says to extract the characters at positions 6, 7, and 8. The problem is, visual basic starts numbering at zero. Therefore, the last three characters of string (s) are at positions 5, 6, and 7. There is no position 8. If we change line 5 to [*ss = s.SubString (5, 3)*], the program will work.

To have a program continue running, instead of just executing the next statement, we can press the (F5) key.

Once we have found the error we can erase the breakpoints by clicking the word (Debug) in the menu bar and then clicking (Delete All Breakpoints).

For our next type of source code statement let's look at a statement we briefly saw in a previous chapter, the (IF) statement.

IF (something) then (do this)

The following lines of code are examples of the basic (IF) statement. The code that follows the (Then) word is done if and only if the (IF) condition is true.

Dim i As Integer = 0 Dim s As String = “AbC”		
If i = 0 Then ... If i < 0 Then ... If i <= 0 Then ...	equals less than less or equal	it is it is not it is
If s = “abc” Then ... If s = “AbC” Then ...		it is not it is
If s IsNot “abc” Then ... If Not s = “abc” Then ... If s <> “abc” Then ...	 not equal	it is it is it is

The symbol for greater than is (>) and the symbol for greater than or equal to is (>=).

MORE SOURCE CODE

The following lines of code can be used if we don't know whether the characters in a string are lower-case or upper-case.

Dim s As String = "AbC"	
If s = "abc" Then ...	it is not
If s.ToUpper = "ABC" Then ...	it is
If String.Compare (s, "abc", True) = 0 Then	True

The following line of code can be used to see if a string contains nothing.

Dim s As String	
If s = "" Then ...	it is

The following lines of code can be used to see if part of a string matches a certain condition.

1	Dim s As String = "AbC"	
2	If s Like "A#C" Then ...	it is not
3	If s Like "A?C" Then ...	it is
4	If s Like "A*" Then ...	it is
5	If IsNumeric (s) Then ...	it is not
6	If Not IsNumeric (s) Then ...	it is
7	If IsDate (s) Then ...	it is not

Line 2 .. True, if the first character is (A), and the second character is any digit from 0 to 9, and the third character is (C).

Line 3 .. True, if the first character is (A), and the second character is any character, and the third character is (C).

Line 4 .. True, if the first character is (A).

Line 5 .. True, if the string contains a valid number.

Line 6 .. True, if the string does not contain a valid number.

Line 7 .. True, if the string contains a valid date.

The following lines of code can be used when we need to check for two conditions.

1	Dim i As Integer = 2	
2	Dim s As String = “AbC”	
3	If (i = 2) And (s = “abc”) Then ...	it is not
4	If (i = 2) Or (s = “abc”) Then ...	it is
5	If (i = 2) And Not (s = “abc”) Then ...	it is

The following lines of code can be used when checking Boolean data types.

Dim Tf As Boolean = True	
If Tf Then ...	True
If Not Tf Then ...	False

If we have several things to do when a condition is true, then we can use the following type of (IF) statement.

```
Dim s As String = “AbC”
If s = “AbC” Then
  do statement 1
  do statement 2
  End If
```

When an (IF) statement contains more than one do-statement the last line has to be an (End If) statement.

If we want to do some things if a condition is true but do some other things if the condition is false, then we can use an (If-Then-Else) statement.

```
Dim s As String = "AbC"
If  s = "AbC"    Then s = "good"    Else s = "bad"
```

```
If s = "AbC"  Then
  do statement 1
  do statement 2
  Else
  do statement 3
  do statement 4
  End if
```

Our next type of statement will allow us to execute a group of statements over and over and over.

LOOPS

There are three basic types of looping statements, (For), (Do-Until), and (Do-While).

For

A (For) loop will allow us to do a series of statements a fixed number of times. The following lines of code will execute a group of statements 10 times.

```
For i As Integer = 1 To 10
   other statements
   Next i
```

A (For) loop must end with a (Next) statement. The following lines of code are variations of the (For) loop.

For i = 1 To 10 Step 2 For i = 5 To 1 Step -1	do for i = 2, 4, 6, 8, and 10 do for i = 5, 4, 3, 2, and 1

The following lines of code show how to abort a (For) loop by using an (Exit For) statement.

```
For i = 1 To 10
   If x = 5   Then Exit For
   x = x + 1
   Next i
```

The following lines of code show how to do a (For) loop, except when a certain condition is true, by using a (Continue For) statement.

```
For i = 1 To 10
   If i = 5   Then Continue For
   statements
   Next i
```

The (For) loop will do the statements 9 times. The statements will not be done when (i = 5).

What if we don't know how many times we need to do a series of statements? There are two types of visual basic looping statements that will do a series of statements (until) a certain condition is true. There are also two types of visual basic looping statements that will do a series of statements (as long as) a certain condition is true.

Do-Until

A (Do-Until) loop allows us to do a series of statements until a certain condition is true. The following lines of code will execute a group of statements until the value of (i) is (5).

```
Do Until i = 5
   i = i + 1
   other statements
   Loop
```

A (Do-Until) loop must end with a (Loop) statement.

The (Until) condition (i = 5) is checked at the (Do) statement. If (i = 5) going into the loop, then the (Do) loop is not performed.

Warning! If (i > 5) going into the loop, or (i) can never become (5) for some other reason, then the (Do) loop will try to execute an infinite number of times.

Like the (For) statement, there is an (Exit) statement and a (Continue) statement that works with a (Do-Until) loop.

```
Do Until i = 5
   If i = 2   Then Continue Do
   If i = 4   Then Exit Do
   other statements
   Loop
```

If (i = 2) then the (other statements) will not be done.
If (i = 4) then the program will abort the (Do Loop).

Do-Loop-Until

A (Do-Loop-Until) is a variation of the (Do-Until) loop.

```
Do
   i = i + 1
   other statements
   Loop Until i = 5
```

A (Do-Loop-Until) is like a (Do-Until) loop except the (Until) condition (i = 5) is checked at the (Loop) statement instead of the (Do) statement. A (Do-Loop-Until) loop will always execute one time.

The (Continue-Do) statement and the (Exit-Do) statement also work with a (Do-Loop-Until) statement.

Do-While

A (Do-Until) loop allows us to do a series of statements (until) a certain condition is true. A (Do-While) loop allows us to do a series of statements (as long as) a certain condition is true. The following lines of code will execute a group of statements as long as the value of (i) is less than (5).

```
Do While i < 5
   i = i + 1
   other statements
   Loop
```

A (Do-While) loop must also end with a (Loop) statement.

The (While) condition (i < 5) is checked at the (Do) statement. If (i) is greater than or equal to (5) going into the loop, then the (Do) loop is not performed.

The (Continue-Do) statement and the (Exit-Do) statement also work with a (Do-While) loop.

```
Do While i < 5
   If i = 2   Then Continue Do
   If i = 4   Then Exit Do
   other statements
   Loop
```

If (i = 2) then the (other statements) will not be done.
If (i = 4) then the program will abort the (Do Loop).

Do-Loop-While

A (Do-Loop-While) is a variation of the (Do-While) loop.

```
Do
   i = i + 1
   other statements
   Loop While i < 5
```

A (Do-Loop-While) is like a (Do-While) loop except the (While) condition (i < 5) is checked at the (Loop) statement instead of the (Do) statement. A (Do-Loop-While) loop will always execute one time.

The (Continue-Do) statement and the (Exit-Do) statement also work with a (Do-Loop-While) loop.

The following is a summary of when a loop condition is checked.

type of loop	when the condition is checked
Do Until	at the (Do) statement
Do - Loop Until	at the (Loop) statement
Do While	at the (Do) statement
Do - Loop while	at the (Loop) statement

Up to this point, we have been using a label or textbox to display the results of our code. If we want to display a more elaborate message to the user we can use a message box.

MESSAGE BOX

Message-Box.Show .. The following lines of code will display the following message box somewhere on the screen.

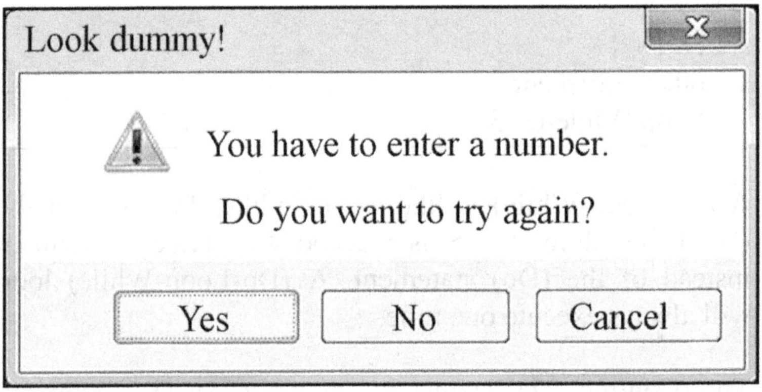

```
Dim IntYesNo As Integer
Dim Caption As String = "Look dummy!"
Dim Message As String = "You have to enter a number."
IntYesNo = MessageBox.Show (Message,  Caption,
   MessageBoxButtons.YesNoCancel,
   MessageBoxIcon.Warning,
   MessageBoxDefaultButton.Button1)
```

Message-Box-Buttons .. Specifies which buttons we want displayed in the message-box. Besides YesNoCancel, we can have OK, OKCancel, AbortRetryIgnore, YesNo, or RetryCancel.

Message-Box-Icon .. Specifies which icon we want displayed in the message-box. Besides Warning, we can have None, Error, Exclamation, Information, Question mark, or Stop.

Message-Box-Default-Button .. Specifies which button is considered pressed if the user just presses the Enter key.

Dialog-Results .. The following line of code can be used to detect which message-box button the user clicks.

```
Dim IntYesNo As Integer
If IntYesNo = DialogResult.Yes   Then ...
```

Beside Yes, we can also check for NO, OK, Abort, Cancel, or Retry.

Suppose we want to pass a message to another program. We can pass a message to another program if we copy the message to the Windows clipboard.

CLIPBOARD

The following lines of code will copy a message to the Windows clipboard.

```
Clipboard.Clear
My.Computer.Clipboard.SetText ("Program worked")
```

We can then paste the message into any program that can accept text from the clipboard, such as Word or Excel. The following line of code can be used to get a message that is waiting in the clipboard.

```
If My.Computer.Clipboard.ContainsText
   Then StringX = My.Computer.Clipboard.GetText
```

Before going on to more advanced coding, let's pause for a second to ponder just how great we are for making it this far.

PAUSING

The following line of code can be used to pause the program for 5 seconds.

```
System.Threading.Thread.Sleep (5000)
```

In this chapter, we covered some of the basic coding statements. More information about these types of statements is available on the internet.

If we do an internet search for "*visual basic 2017 IF statement*", we can find websites and videos that show us more information on how to use the (IF) statement.

We have now learned a lot of source code, and yet the programs we can write are elementary. In the next chapter, we will learn some advanced coding techniques that will make our programs look and act like real programs.

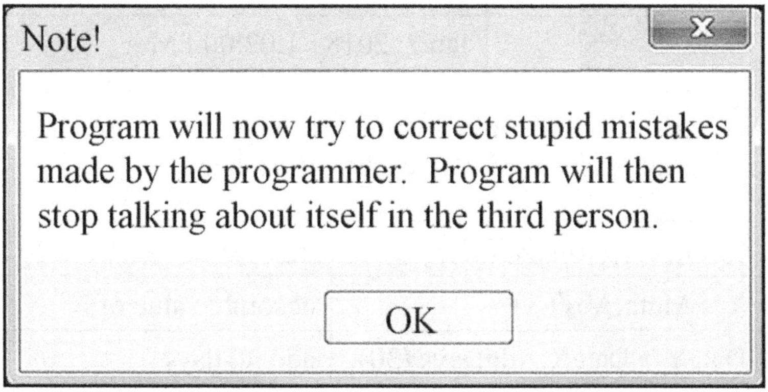

==

Chapter 7
ADVANCED CODING

In the previous chapter, we learned about different types of data.

Strings	“”, “aBc”, “-3.14”
Numbers	Integer, Long, Single, Double
Boolean	True, False
Date	Jan 2, 2018, 1:02:00 PM

We also learned about different types of source code statements associated with each type of data.

StringY = StringX.ToUpper	convert to upper-case
Y = Math.Abs (X)	absolute value of X
DateY = DateX.AddDays (30)	add 30 days

And we learned about some of the more common general-purpose source code statements such as

```
'check to see if variable (s) is equal to string "abc".
If s = "abc"   Then ...
```

```
'do a series of statements 10 times.
For i = 1 To 10
   statements
   Next i
```

```
'do a series of statements until a condition is true.
Do Until i = 5
   statements
   Loop
```

```
'do a series of statements as long as something is true.
Do While i < 5
   statements
   Loop
```

```
'display a message box on the screen.
IntYesNo = MessageBox.Show (Message,  Caption,
```

```
'copy something to the Windows clipboard.
My.Computer.Clipboard.SetText ("Program worked")
```

```
'pause the program for 5 seconds.
System.Threading.Thread.Sleep (5000)
```

In this chapter, we will look at the source code needed to perform more complicated tasks such as

Work with text files.
Work with databases.
Print a report.
Run our program without using visual studio.

Before we dig into the hard stuff, let's learn how to add additional forms to our program.

FORMS

Most programs are like the visual studio IDE program we use to write our own programs. Visual studio has a (get-started) form, a (form-design) form for designing how we want our program to look, and a (coding) form where we write the source code that makes the program work. Each form has a different appearance and function. Our (Controls) program has only one form called (Form1). Let's add a second form to our Controls program where we can do some advanced coding. To add a second form to the Controls program we can do the following.

1 .. Click the (Form1.vb design) tab to display Form1.

2 .. Click the word (Project) in the menu bar and then click (Add Windows Form). This will bring up the (Add New Item) window.

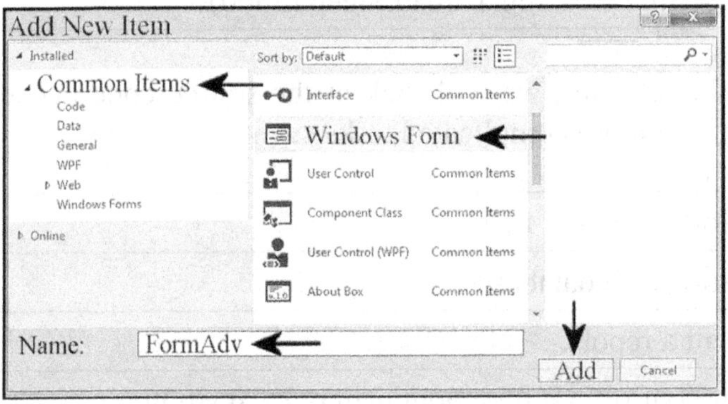

3 .. In the left frame, select (Installed) and then select (Common-Items). In the center frame, select (Windows Form). For (Name), let's name our second form (FormAdv.vb). When done, click the (Add) button.

Once the second form has been added to the program we can set the properties of the form.

FormBorderStyle .. Let's add a border to the advanced form by setting this property to (Fixed single).

Text .. We can use this property to specify the words that appear in the title bar of the advanced form. Let's set the title bar text property to (Advanced stuff).

There should now be three tabs at the top of the form-design frame.

Form1.vb design .. The form-design frame for the main form.

Form1.vb .. The coding frame that goes with the main form.

FormAdv.vb design .. The form-design frame for the advanced form.

To create the coding frame for our second form just click the (FormAdv.vb design) tab and then double-click anywhere inside the form. This will create the (FormAdv.vb) frame and the (FormAdv-Load) subroutine.

For our two-form program to work, we need source code that will switch from Form1 to FormAdv and back again.

Show .. The following line of code will display the advanced form when we click a Button1 control on the main form. This line of code goes in the Form1 Button1-click subroutine.

```
Public Class Form1
Private Sub Button1-Click (
   FormAdv.Show ( )
```

When we test the program and click the Button1 control to display the second form we may find that the second form does not display exactly on top of the main form.

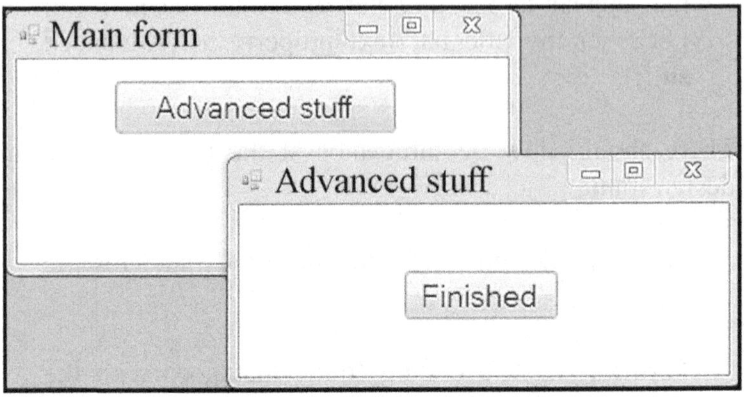

If we want the advanced form to display exactly on top of the main form, we can put the following lines of code in the (FormAdv-Load) event of the advanced form.

```
Public Class FormAdv
Private Sub FormAdv-Load (
   Me.Location = Form1.Location
   Me.Size = Form1.Size
```

Hide .. The following line of code will hide the advanced form and redisplay the main form when we click a button control on the advanced form or click the (x) in the upper-right corner of the advanced form.

```
Public Class FormAdv
Private Sub Button1-Click (
   Me.Hide ( )
```

The controls and variables we put on the second form are independent of the controls and variables we have on the main form. The button control on the main form and the button control on the second form can both be called Button1.

For our first advanced coding topic let's look at ways we can store and reuse a large amount of data.

FILES AND FOLDERS

Before we look at how to store data in a file let's look at some source code that manages the files and folders that exist on a Windows computer. A lot of the source code has already been written and stored in a library of source code called (System.IO). All we need to do is add this library to each form in our program that works with files.

Imports .. The following line of code will add the System.IO library of pre-written code to the second form of our program. This line of code needs to be the first line of code in each form that works with files.

```
Imports System.IO
Public Class FormAdv
```

Once the System.IO library of code has been added to the form we can use the library's code to work with files and folders. We will not actually see the pre-written source code that is contained in the System.IO library but the code is there for us to use.

Directory-Exists .. The following line of code will tell us if a certain folder exists on a computer.

```
If Directory.Exists ("C:\FolderX")   then ...
```

Unlike string statements, file and folder statements are not case sensitive. It does not matter whether we check for (FolderX) or (FOLDERx).

Create-Directory .. The following line of code will create a new folder called (MyFolder).

```
Directory.CreateDirectory ("C:\MyFolder")
```

Copy-Directory .. The following line of code will copy a folder, and all its contents, from one location to a different location.

```
My.Computer.FileSystem.CopyDirectory ( _
   "C:\FolderX", "C:\FolderY")
```

Move .. The following line of code will change the name of a folder to a different name.

```
Directory.Move ("C:\FolderX",  "C:\FolderY")
```

Delete .. The following lines of code will delete a file and then delete the empty folder that contained the file.

```
File.Delete ("C:\FolderX\FileY.txt")
Directory.Delete ("C:\FolderX")
```

The following examples show how to work with the files on a computer.

File-Exists .. The following line of code will tell us if a certain file exists on a computer.

```
If File.Exists ("C:\FolderX\FileX.txt")  then ...
```

Copy-File .. The following line of code will copy a file from one location to a different location.

```
File.Copy ("C:\FolderX\Fx.txt", "C:\FolderY\Fy.txt")
```

Rename .. The following line of code will change the name and location of a file to a different name and location.

```
Rename ("C:\FolderY\Fy.txt", "C:\FolderZ\Fz.txt")
```

Delete .. The following line of code will delete a file.

```
File.Delete ("C:\FolderZ\Fz.txt")
```

Now that we know how to work with the files and folders on a computer, let's see how to store data in a text file.

TEXT FILES

Earlier we worked with a list-view table that contained the name, age, and family-status of three people. Suppose we manage to collect data for several hundred relatives. There are two ways to store large amounts of data, in a file or in a database. Let's look at how to store the data in a text file.

text file (C:\MyFolder\MyFile.txt)
Larry, 25, Yes Mary, 35, No Terry, 45, ???

The following lines of code will write the three list-view records to a text file called (MyFile.txt). The text file will be stored in an existing folder (C:\MyFolder).

```
Dim MyFile As String = "C:\MyFolder\MyFile.txt"
Dim MyWriter As New StreamWriter (MyFile)
Dim s As String
s = "Larry"   & ", "   & "25"   & ", "   & "Yes"
MyWriter.WriteLine (s)
s = "Mary"   & ", "   & "35"   & ", "   & "No"
MyWriter.WriteLine (s)
s = "Terry"   & ", "   & "45"   & ", "   & "???"
MyWriter.WriteLine (s)
MyWriter.Close ( )
```

If any of the fields contain a comma then a different character can be used to separate the field. We can check to see if the program worked by locating the file on our computer and double-clicking the name of the file. The file should open up in Notepad.

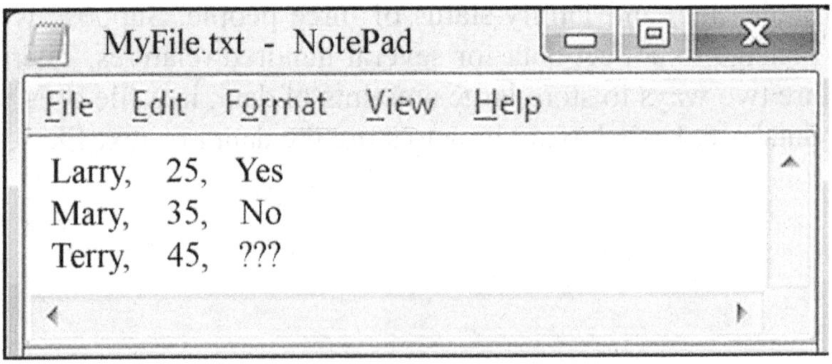

If we have hundreds of records to save to a text file, it is easier to store the data in three separate arrays and then use the following code to save the data to a text file.

```
For i = 1 to 500
   s = Name (i)  & ", "  & Age (i)  & ", "  & Family (i)
   MyWriter.WriteLine (s)
   Next i
```

The following lines of code can be used to add a fourth record to an existing text file.

```
Dim MyFile As String = "C:\MyFolder\MyFile.txt"
Dim MyWriter As New StreamWriter (MyFile, True)
s = "Jerry"  & ", "  & "5"  & ", "  & "Yes"
MyWriter.WriteLine (s)
MyWriter.Close ( )
```

The following lines of code will read the records we previously stored in the text file (C:\MyFolder\MyFile.txt).

```
Dim MyFile As String = "C:\MyFolder\MyFile.txt"
Dim ss ( ) As String
FileOpen (1, MyFile, OpenMode.Input)
Do Until EOF (1)  '-- do until end of file
    s = LineInput (1)
    ss = Split (s, ",") '-- split string separated by commas
    Name = ss (0)  :  Age = ss (1)  :  Family = ss (2)
    Loop
FileClose (1)
```

Any line, or part of a line, that starts with an apostrophe (') is a comment and will not be executed by the program. We can put several short statements on the same line by separating the statements with a colon (:).

The first line of code defines the name and location of the file we want to read. If we don't know the name or location of the file we can use the following procedure to display the standard locate-and-open windows dialog box.

OPEN FILE DIALOG BOX

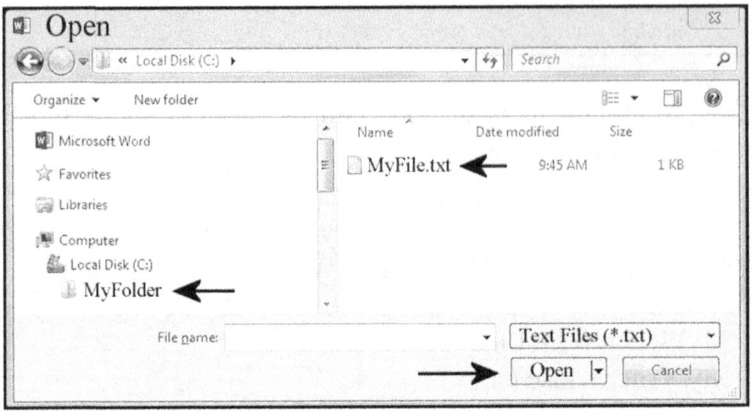

For our program to display the standard locate-and-open windows dialog box, we need to add a new control to the program.

OpenFileDialog control .. This control is in the (Dialogs) group of the toolbox controls. Like the Timer control, when we drag the OpenFileDialog control from the Toolbox to the form design window the control icon shows up at the bottom of the design frame.

The following lines of code will display the locate-and-open windows dialog box.

```
Dim MyFile As String
With OpenFileDialog1
   .FileName = ""
   .Filter = "text-files | *.txt"
   .InitialDirectory = "C:\"
   .Title = "Locate file to open"
   End With
OpenFileDialog1.ShowDialog ( )
MyFile = OpenFileDialog1.FileName
```

The (Filter) line will cause the locate-and-open window to display only (.txt) text files.

The last line of code sets the string (MyFile) to the name and location of the file we want to read, (C:\MyFolder\MyFile.txt).

After we identify the name and location of the text file we want to open and read we can use the previous code to read the records in the file.

Besides the OpenFile dialog window we can also have our program display the standard (Save-File), (Choose-Font), or (Choose-Color) dialog boxes.

There is a better way to store large amounts of data than storing the data in a file.

DATABASES

The second way to store large amounts of data is in a database. The advantage of storing data in a database is that we can retrieve a particular record without having to read all the records that precede it. Due to the complexity of a database, more code is required to work with the data in a database than to work with data stored in a file. We can use the following procedure to create a database called (MyDb) and store it in the existing folder (C:\MyFolder).

First, we need to use the (Import) statement to add 3 libraries of pre-written code to the program. These lines of code need to be at the top of each form that works with databases.

```
Imports System.Data
Imports System.Data.Sql
Imports System.Data.OleDb
Public Class FormAdv
```

Once the libraries have been added to the form we can use their code to work with databases. We will not actually see the pre-written source code that is contained in the libraries but the code is there for us to use.

The following lines of code will create the MyDb database.

```
Dim cat As ADOX.Catalog = New ADOX.Catalog
cat.Create ("Provider=Microsoft.Jet.OLEDB.4.0;" &
   "Data Source=C:\MyFolder\MyDb.mdb")

Dim ConnectionString As String =
   "Provider=Microsoft.Jet.OLEDB.4.0;" &
   "Data Source=" & "C:\MyFolder\MyDb.mdb"
Dim DbConnection As New OleDb.OleDbConnection (
    ConnectionString)
DbConnection.Open ( )

'-- Continued on next page
```

```
'-- Continued from previous page
Dim Table As New ADOX.Table
Table.Name = "FamilyTable"
Table.Columns.Append (
   "Name", ADOX.DataTypeEnum.adVarWChar, 50)
Table.Columns.Append (
   "Age", ADOX.DataTypeEnum.adInteger)
Table.Columns.Append (
   "Family", ADOX.DataTypeEnum.adVarWChar, 10)
cat.Tables.Append (Table)
DbConnection.Close ( )
```

When we run the program, it will create a database called (MyDb.mdb) in folder (C:\MyFolder). The database will not contain any data. Unlike a text file, we cannot double-click the name of a database and have it open up, unless we have the Microsoft Access program, which is part of the Microsoft's Office Professional package.

The following examples show how to work with the MyDb database. All of the following examples require the following lines of code at the beginning of the routine.

```
'-- Statements required for each database routine
Dim SqlString As String
Dim ConnectionString As String =
   "Provider=Microsoft.Jet.OLEDB.4.0;" &
   "Data Source=" & "C:\MyFolder\MyDb.mdb"
Dim DbConnection As New OleDb.OleDbConnection (
    ConnectionString)
DbConnection.Open ( )
```

We can use the following lines of code to add a record to the database. Be sure to include the statements required for each database routine.

```
'-- Include statements required for each database routine
Dim Name, Age, Family As String
Name = "Larry"  :  Age = 25  :  Family = "Yes"
Dim StringFieldValues As String
Dim StringFields As String = "(Name, Age, Family)"
StringFieldValues = _
    "Values ( " & _
    " ' "   & TheirName    & " ', "   & _
    " ' "   & TheirAge     & " ', "   & _
    " ' "   & TheirFamily  & " ' )"
Dim AddCmdStr As String =
   "INSERT INTO FamilyTable " &
    StringFields & StringFieldValues
Dim AddCmd As New OleDb.OleDbCommand (
   AddCmdStr, DbConnection)
AddCmd.ExecuteNonQuery ( )
DbConnection.Close ( )
```

The following lines of code will count the number of records in the database.

```
'-- Include statements required for each database routine
Dim NumberOfDbRecords As Integer
SqlString = "SELECT count (*) FROM FamilyTable"
Dim DbCommand As New OleDb.OleDbCommand (
   SqlString, DbConnection)
NumberOfDbRecords =
   CLng (DbCommand.ExecuteScalar)
DbConnection.Close ( )
```

The following lines of code will read the database records.

```
'-- Include statements required for each database routine
Dim Name, Age, Family As String
SqlString = "SELECT * FROM FamilyTable"
Dim DbCommand As New OleDb.OleDbCommand (
   SqlString, DbConnection)
Dim DbDataReader As OleDbDataReader =
   DbCommand.ExecuteReader ( )
While DbDataReader.Read
   Name = DbDataReader("Name")
   Age = DbDataReader("Age").ToString
   Family = DbDataReader("Family")
   End While
DbDataReader.Close ( )
DbConnection.Close ( )
```

The following lines of code will search for and read one record from the database.

```
'-- Include statements required for each database routine
Dim Name, Age, Family As String
SqlString = "SELECT * FROM FamilyTable
   WHERE Name = 'Mary' "
Dim DbCommand As New OleDb.OleDbCommand (
   SqlString, DbConnection)
Dim DbDataReader As OleDbDataReader =
   DbCommand.ExecuteReader ( )
While DbDataReader.Read
   Name = DbDataReader("Name")
   Age = DbDataReader("Age").ToString
   Family = DbDataReader("Family")
   End While
DbDataReader.Close ( )
DbConnection.Close ( )
```

The only difference between reading all the records and reading a selected record is the (SqlString =) statement.

The following lines of code can be used to delete a record from the database.

```
'-- Include statements required for each database routine
Dim Name2delete As String = "Mary"
Dim DelCmdStr As String =
   "DELETE FROM FamilyTable " &
   "WHERE Name = ' " & Name2delete & " ' "
Dim DelCmd As New OleDb.OleDbCommand (
   DelCmdStr, DbConnection)
DelCmd.ExecuteNonQuery ( )
DbConnection.Close ( )
```

The routines above are just a small part of what can be done with databases. The (Sql) in the (SqlString =) statements stands for (Structured Query Language). SQL is a small programming language that was created just to work with databases.

Almost all of the database routines require the same 4 statements at the beginning of the routine. There is a way to write a section of code and execute the code from anywhere in the program.

SUBROUTINES

A *subroutine* is a block of code that we can execute from anywhere in the program by using a (Call) statement.

The following lines of code is a subroutine that will extract the character at position (i) from string (s).

```
Private Sub MySub (
   s As String,    i As Integer,    ByRef Ans As String)
   '-------------------------------------------------------------
   Ans = s.Substring (i, 1)
   other lines of code
   End Sub
```

From anywhere in the program we can use the following line of code to extract the character at position (x) from string (StringX). The answer will be in variable (CharX).

```
Call MySub (StringX,  x,  CharX)
```

The subroutine, and the statements that calls the subroutine, must contain the same number of variables, in this case 3. The names of the variables do not need to match but they do have to be of the same data type. The first and third variables must be strings and the second variable must be an integer.

In the (Private Sub MySub) line, the third variable (Ans) is preceded by the word (ByRef).

Without ByRef .. Variables (s) and (i) are copies of variables (StringX) and (x). If the subroutine changes the value of (s) or (i), the value of (StringX) or (x) does not change.

With ByRef .. Variable (Ans) is the variable (CharX). If the subroutine changes the value of (Ans), the value of (CharX) also changes.

It is the programmer's choice as to whether to pass a variable ByRef or not.

The real value of using a subroutine is when the subroutine contains several lines of code that perform a complex function, and the subroutine is called from several locations throughout the program.

VARIABLES

Variables are an integral part of any program. They are also a common cause of program bugs. The following is a summary of some of the rules regarding the use of variables.

All variables must be declared before they are used. Where and how to declare a variable is very important. We now have three different ways to define a variable, a (Dim) statement, a (Private) statement, and a (Public) statement.

Dim StringD as String .. The value of StringD is known only inside the routine where it is defined.

```
Public Class Form1
Private Sub MySub ( )
   Dim StringD as String = "abc"
   End Sub
Private Sub Button1-Click (
   Dim StringD as String = "x"
   End Sub
```

The StringD in subroutine MySub and the StringD in Button1-Click are two different variables. If StringD is defined inside a (For) or (Do) loop, then its value is known only inside the loop.

Private StringPri as String .. The value of StringPri is known in every routine in the form.

```
Public Class Form1
   Private StringPri as string = "abc"
Private Sub MySub ( )
   Dim StringD as String = StringPri
   End Sub
Private Sub Button1-Click (
   Dim StringD as String = StringPri
   End Sub
```

The value of StringPri is known in subroutine MySub and in Button1-Click. StringPri is also known inside a (For) or (Do) loop. Private variables must be defined at the top of the form.

Public StringPub as String .. The value of StringPub is known in every form of the program. Changing the value of StringPub anywhere in FormAdv will change its value in Form1.

Public variables, also called global variables, must be defined in a separate form called a *module*. We can add a module to our program by doing the following.

Click the word (Project) in the menu bar and then click (Add Module). This will bring up the (Add New Item) window.

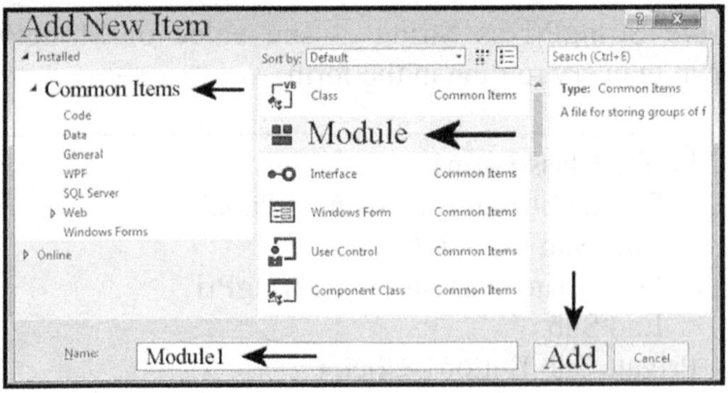

In the left frame, select (Common Items). In the middle frame, select (Module).

Give the module a name and then click (Add).

We can now define Public variables that are accessible anywhere in the program.

```
Module Module1
   Public StringPub As String
End Module
```

```
Public Class Form1
   StringPub = "abc"
```

```
Public Class FormAdv
   Label2.Text = StringPub
```

Besides defining a public global variable, we can also put a public global subroutine in the module. The subroutine can then be called from any form in the program.

```
Module Module1
Public Sub MySub (s as String)
   subroutine code
   End Sub
End Module
```

PRINTING

For visual basic to be so powerful, printing a few lines on the printer may seem overly complicated. To print, we need to add one, and possibly two, new controls to our program.

PrintDocument control .. This control is needed to design and print one page. The control is located in the (Printing) group of the toolbox controls. Like the Timer control, when we drag the PrintDocument control to the form design window it shows up at the bottom of the form.

PrintPreviewControl .. This control is needed if we want to see what a printed page will look like prior to printing it. This control is also in the (Printing) group of the toolbox controls. Make the size of the control big enough to see what a printed page will look like.

Start by double-clicking the PrintDocument control located at the bottom of the design frame. This will create the (PrintDocument1-PrintPage) subroutine.

The following lines of code, put in the (PrintDocument1-PrintPage) subroutine, will design one page of printed output which consists of two lines.

```
Private Sub PrintDocument1-PrintPage (e As Printing.Pri
Dim StringX As String = "Line 2 .. ABCDEF"
Dim MyFont As Font = New Drawing.Font (
   "Times New Roman", 16)
e.Graphics.DrawString (
   "Line 1", MyFont, Brushes.Red, 100.0, 100.0)
MyFont = New Drawing.Font (
   "Lucida Handwriting", 20, FontStyle.Bold)
e.Graphics.DrawString (
   StringX, MyFont, Brushes.Blue, 150.0, 200.0)
```

We have to use the (e.Graphics.DrawString) statement to describe each line we want to print on the page. The (Brushes) parameter allows us to specify the color of the text we want to print. The two integers, 100 and 100, specify how far over (x), and how far down (y), to skip before printing the line. a value of 100 is about one inch.

The following line of code, located somewhere else in the program, will let us see what a printed page will look like prior to printing it.

```
PrintPreviewControl1.Document = PrintDocument1
```

The following lines of code, located somewhere else in the program, will print the page.

```
PrintDocument1.PrinterSettings.Copies = 1
PrintDocument1.DefaultPageSettings.Landscape = True
PrintDocument1.Print ( )
```

Printing a report that consists of several pages is even harder. The following lines of code will design one 2-line page of the report.

```
Public Class FormAdv
   Private Line1string, Line2string As String
'------------------------------------------------------------
Private Sub PrintDocument1-PrintPage (e As Printing.Pri
Dim MyFont As Font = New Drawing.Font (
   "Times New Roman", 16)
e.Graphics.DrawString (
   Line1string, MyFont, Brushes.Black, 100.0, 100.0)
e.Graphics.DrawString (
   Line2string, MyFont, Brushes.Black, 150.0, 200.0)
```

The following lines of code, located somewhere else in the program, will print the report.

```
Line1string = "Page-1 Line-1"
Line2string = "Page-1 Line-2"
PrintDocument1.Print ( )
Line1string = "Page-2 Line-1"
Line2string = "Page-2 Line-2"
PrintDocument1.Print ( )
```

Let's end the chapter by going back to that first program we wrote, the Hello program. If we plan to run our Hello program several times, then it would be nice if we could run the program without having to first load the program into visual studio.

CREATING AN INSTALL FILE

The solution is to create a program called (setup.exe). When we run the setup.exe program it will create a symbol on our desktop called a shortcut. After that, we can run our Hello program by double-clicking the desktop Hello Program shortcut. We won't have to load the Hello program into visual studio to run it. Prior to creating a setup program, we need to run the Hello program to make sure it works the way we want it to.

In some cases, we have to download an additional program from the internet in order to create a setup program. To see if we need to download an additional program we can do the following.

With the Hello program loaded into visual studio, click the word (File) in the menu bar and then click (Add) and then click (New Project). This will bring up the (Add New Project) window.

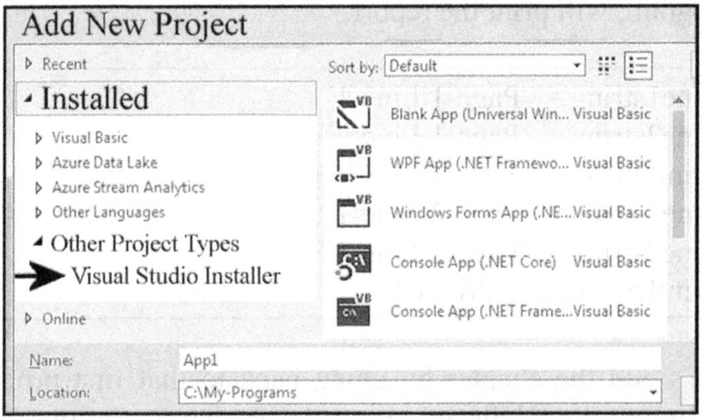

In the left frame, open the category called (Installed).

In the Installed category there should be an (Other Project Types) category which contains a (Visual Studio Installer) line.

If the Visual Studio Installer is missing, we can install it from the internet by doing the following.

> If we do an internet search for "*visual basic 2017 installer projects*", we can find a website where we can download the Visual Studio Installer program.

The following download screen is from the website *https://marketplace.visualstudio.com/items?itemName=VisualStudioClient.MicrosoftVisualStudio2017InstallerProjects*

Click (Download) to download the file (*InstallerProjects.vsix*). The file extension (vsix) stands for Visual Studio Extension Installer.

The documentation referenced on this download website appears to be out of date.

After the (InstallerProjects.vsix) file has been downloaded, close visual studio.

Go to where the InstallerProjects file was downloaded and double-click (InstallerProjects.vsix). The installation should display the following screens.

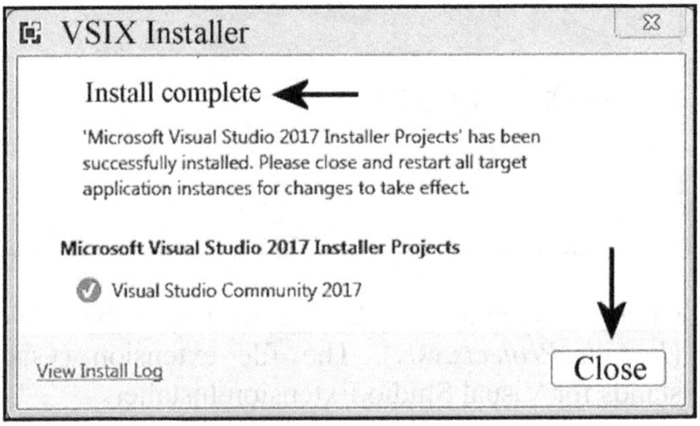

When the installation is finished, run visual studio and reload the Hello program.

We are now ready to create a setup program for our Hello program. This is a complicated process. It is probably a good idea to search the internet for recent videos of "*visual studio 2017 how to create setup.exe*".

The first step is to create a (Setup Project).

With the Hello program loaded into visual studio, click the word (File) in the menu bar and then click (Add) and then click (New Project). This will bring up the (Add New Project) window.

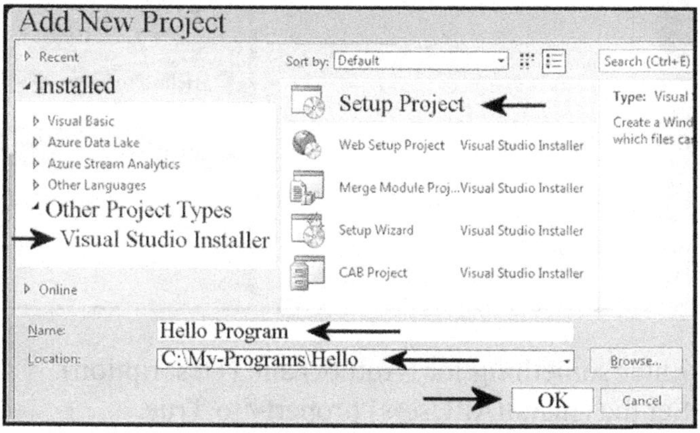

On the left side, under (Installed), select (Visual Studio Installer). In the middle frame, select (Setup Project).

For (Name), let's enter (Hello Program). The file name of the setup program will still be setup.exe, but the name of the installation process will be Hello Program.

For (Location), enter the name of the folder where we saved the Hello program, which is probably (C:\My-Programs\Hello).

Click Ok. This will add a [File System (Hello Program)] tab to the visual studio form.

The next step is to set some of the properties of the setup project by clicking (Hello Program) in the (Solution Explorer) frame.

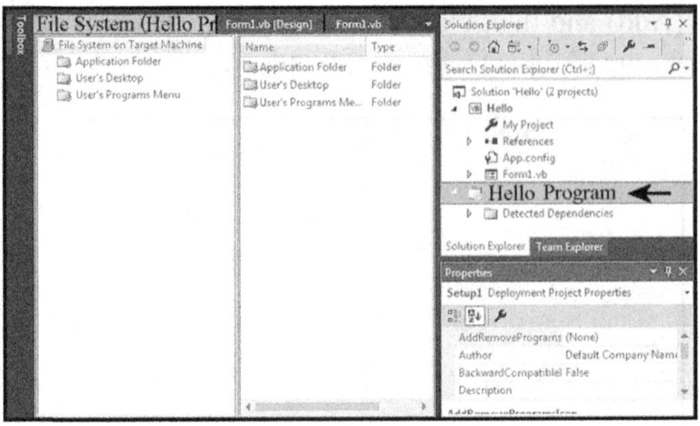

Enter something for (Author) and (Description).
Set the (InstallAllUsers) property to True.
Set the (Manufacturer) line to one space character.
Enter something for (ProductName).
Set (RemovePreviousVersions) to True.

The next step is to create an (Application Folder) on our computer. This is where the setup program will end up. In the left frame, under the (File System Hello) tab, right-click the (Application Folder) line. Select (Add) and then click (Project Output). This will bring up the (Add Project Output Group) window.

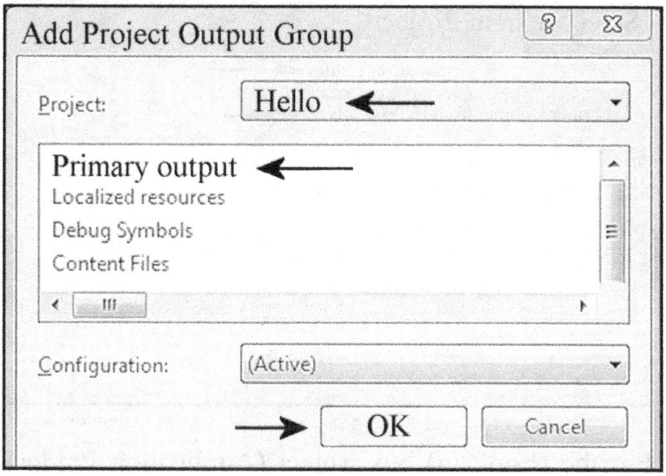

In the (Project) box of the Add Project Output Group window, select the name of the program, which is (Hello). Select (Primary Output) and then click (OK).

With the (Application Folder) line selected, the center frame will now contain a Primary output line and a System.Net line.

The next step is to create a shortcut icon that will appear on the desktop. Once we run the setup.exe program we can run the Hello program by double-clicking the desktop shortcut icon.

In the left frame, under the (File System Hello) tab, select the (User's Desktop) line. Right-click in a blank area of the center frame and select (Create New Shortcut). This will bring up a (Select Item in Project) window.

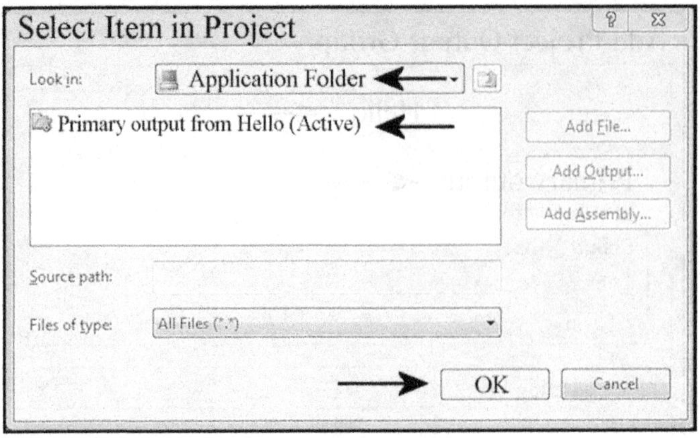

For the (Look in) box, select (Application Folder). Select the (Primary output) line and then click (OK).

With the (User's Desktop) line selected, the center frame will now contain a (Shortcut to Primary Output) line.

Click the (Shortcut to Primary Output) line in the center frame and change the name to (Hello Program).

The next step is to pick the icon that will go with the program shortcut symbol on the desktop.

In the left frame, under the (File System Hello) tab, select the (Application Folder) line.

Right-click in a blank area of the center frame and select (Add) and then select (File).

Locate and select the (.ico) icon file that we want to associate with the program shortcut symbol on the desktop and then click (Open).

With the (Application Folder) line selected, the center frame will now show the name of the selected icon.

In the left frame, under the (File System Hello) tab, select the (User's Desktop) line.

In the center frame, right-click the (Hello Program) line and select (Properties Window). In the Properties frame on the right side of the form do the following.

> Click on the right side of the (Icon) property line and then click the down-arrow and then click (Browse). This will bring up the (Icon) window.

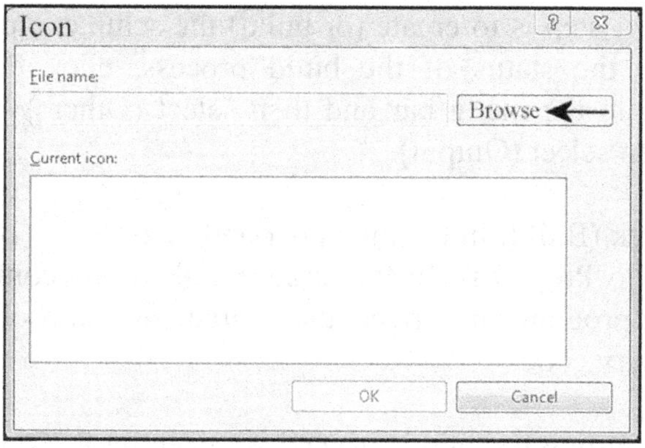

In the (Icon) window, click (Browse). This will bring up the (Select Item in Project) window again.

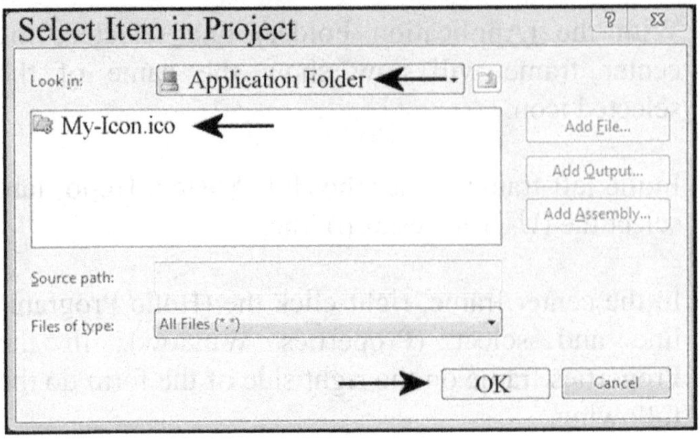

For the (Look in) box, select (Application Folder). Click the icon line and then click (OK). Back on the icon screen, click the icon symbol and then click (OK).

The next step is to create (or build) the setup.exe program. To see the status of the build process, click the word (View) in the menu bar and then select (Other Windows) and then select (Output).

Click (Build) in the menu bar and then select (Build Hello Program). In this case, build means compile the program or convert the source code into object binary code.

Assuming the build succeeded, meaning there were no program bugs, click (Build) in the menu bar and then select (Clean Solution).

Next, click (Build) in the menu bar and then select (Build Solution). In this case, build means create the setup program.

If the build succeeds, we will have our setup.exe program. The setup.exe program will be in folder *C:\My-Programs\Hello\Hello Program\Debug.* There won't be a desktop shortcut icon until we run the setup program.

Up to this point, the Hello program was built into the visual studio program. The last step is to double-click or run the setup.exe program. When we run the setup program it will install the Hello program on our computer making it independent of visual studio. The installation process will also create an icon on our desktop called a shortcut.

From now on, we can run our Hello program by double-clicking the desktop Hello Program icon. It does not matter whether the visual studio program is running or not.

It should be noted that when we are in visual studio and we click the word (File) in the menu bar to close our Hello program, the item (Close Project) has been replaced with (Close Solution).

We can now run our Hello program on our computer by double-clicking the desktop Hello Program icon, but no one else will be able to run our program or their computer even if we give them the setup.exe program. For other people to be able to run our program or their computer the program has to go through a process called *deployment* or *publishing.* Due to the complexities of publishing a program so that other people can install it on their computer, I will leave that topic as homework.

We have now covered about 5 percent of the power of visual studio and visual basic. But even the basics of visual basic will allow us to write our own computer programs. Not just a simple Hello program but sophisticated programs that can perform complicated tasks.

We can learn the theory of music but that does not mean we will know how to compose a symphony. We can learn a lot about grammar and spelling but that does not mean we will know how to write a novel. Likewise, we can learn visual basic but that does not mean we will know how to write a sophisticated computer program. There are two additional things that might make writing your first major program a little easier.

1 .. A good clear comprehensive idea of what you want your program to do.

2 .. Access to the internet where you can ask "how do I do this in visual basic?".

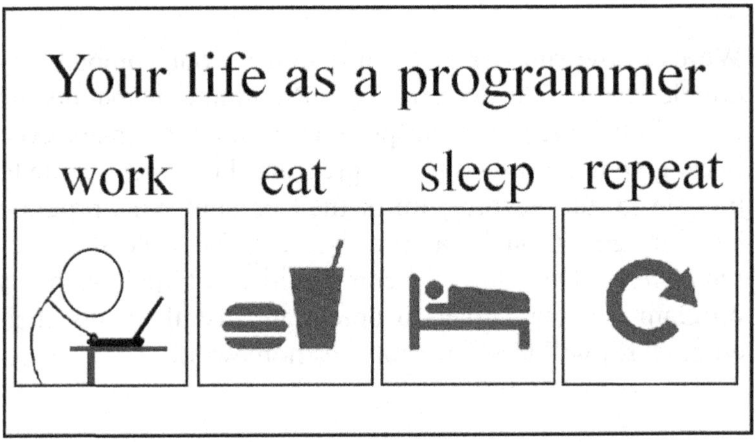

Index

===

About the author

===

Although I have a Master's degree in Mathematics, I have spent my entire post-college life writing computer programs. I wrote my first computer program in 1959 on a Burroughs 205 Datatron vacuum tube mainframe computer which was as big as a small mobile home. By the time I was writing software for aeronautical engineers in the late 1960s, technology had improved to the point where a disk drive was the size of a washing machine. In the mid-1980s, I started my own software development company writing custom software for different types of businesses. In 2000, at age 60, I sold my software company and started writing programs for my hobby, ham radio. One of my current computer programs can be found by doing an internet search on my ham radio call sign which is WA0H (0 is the number zero). Even at age 77 I still write and try to sell my software. From time to time, whenever I needed a little variety in my life, I would teach evening classes in mathematics, statistics, and computer programming at different universities. I live with my wife of 53 years, Joan, who is a retired science teacher.

In 2018, I took a break from programming and wrote a math book called "*Calm Down! It's Only Math*". I wrote the easy-to-read and humorous math book for people who want to relearn all the math they had in school but have long since forgotten.

===

Made in the USA
Monee, IL
04 November 2026

67380395R00125